The Three Lives
Of the
USS DRUM

By

Thomas M. Bowser
A Submarine Veteran Volunteer

The Three Lives of the USS Drum SS-228

Copyright © by Thomas M. Bowser 2013

ISBN 978-0-9893833-0-1

For all those that contributed to building such a fine vessel

To all those that went to war with her
And their families

To all those that trained on her

And especially
For Lesley and all the pieces of cake we have shared

A special thanks to Rosamond Rice, the daughter of the first of Drum's Captains, for her great job of proof reading this book. All remaining errors and/or omissions are wholey mine.

Table of Contents:

Submarine Losses	iii
Prologue	iv
The First Life: The Beginning	1
First Patrol	9
Second Patrol	17
Third Patrol	23
Fourth Patrol	29
Fifth Patrol	35
Sixth Patrol	41
Seventh Patrol	47
Eighth Patrol	53
Ninth Patrol	59
Tenth Patrol	65
Eleventh Patrol	71
Twelfth Patrol	79
Thirteenth Patrol	85
Fourteenth Patrol	91
WWII Crew List	95
The Second Life: The Reserve Period	103
The Third Life: The Restoration:	105
2005	109
2006	113
2007	122
2008	133
2009	145
2010	162
2011	177
2012	203
2013	227

Submarine Losses

The occupation of submarining has always been hazardous; we have lost a total of sixty five submarines since 1900, usually with all hands but occasionally without loss of life. Nine were lost before WWII, four after the war. During WWII we lost fifty two, one out of five that went to sea did not come back. Four ran aground and could not be freed, 1 collided with an escort on the way to Panama Canal, two were lost in training exercises, and two were lost to friendly fire and two by a circular run of their own torpedoes.

Submarine	Date	Cause	Casualties
USS F-4 SS-23	3/25/1915	battery gas, lost depth control, Hawaii	21 men, all hands
USS F-1 SS-20	12/17/1917	collision w/ F-3 SS-22 off Calif.	19 men lost
USS H-1 SS-28	3/20/1920	ran aground, later sank, off Baja	4 men lost
USS S-5 SS-110	9/1/1920	lost on trials	no loss of life
USS O-5 SS-68	10/29/1923	collision SS Ababgarez off Panama Canal	3 men lost
USS S-51 SS-162	9/25/1925	collision w/SS City of Rome off Block Is.	32 men lost
USS S-4 SS-109	12/17/1927	collision w/ USCG Paulding	34 men lost
USS Squalus SS-192	5/29/1939	flooding from induction valve test dive	26 lost 33 rescued
USS O-9 SS-70	6/20/1941	ran aground off Portsmouth	34 men lost
USS Sealion SS-195	12/10/1941	scuttled Manila Bay after bomb damage	no loss of life
USS S-36 SS-141	1/20/1942	ran aground on 2nd patrol	no loss of life
USS S-26 SS-131	1/24/1942	rammed by USS PC-460 2nd patrol	46 men lost 3 survivors
USS Shark SS-174	2/11/1942	depth charged 1st patrol	59 Men lost
USS Perch SS-176	3/3/1942	DC, scuttled 1st patrol, Java	61 crew captured, 53 survi
USS S-27 SS-132	6/19/1942	ran aground in Aleutians	no loss of life
USS Grunion SS-216	7/8/1942	near Kiska Harbor 1st patrol	70 men lost
USS S-39 SS-144	8/16/1942	ran aground	no loss of life
USS Argonaut SS-166	1/10/1943	depth charged near Rabaul 3rd patrol	105 men lost
USS Amberjack SS-219	2/16/1943	depth charged near Rabaul 3rd patrol	72 men lost
USS Grampus SS-207	3/5/1943	surface gun fire 6th patrol Vella Gulf	72 men lost
USS Triton SS-201	3/15/1943	surface gun fire Admiralty Islands	74 men lost
USS Pickerel SS-177	4/3/1943	possible mines 7th patrol off Japan	74 men lost
USS Grenadier SS-210	4/22/1943	bombed, scuttled 6th patrol	61 captured 57 survived
USS Runner SS-275	6/26/-7/4/1943	possible mine, 3rd patrol	78 men lost
USS R-12 SS-89	6/12/1943	flooding on training dive, Key West	42 men lost 3 survived
USS Pompano SS-181	8/29/1943	possible mine, 7th patrol	76 men lost
USS Grayling SS-209	9/12/1943	near Tablas St. 8th patrol	76 men lost
USS Cisco SS-290	9/28/1943	near Mindanao 1st patrol	76 men lost
USS S-44 SS-155	10/7/1943	surface gun fire, Kuriles 5th patrol	56 men lost, 2 survived

Submarine	Date	Cause/Location	Casualties
USS Wahoo SS-238	10/11/1943	air depth charged, 7th patrol, La Perouse St.	79 men
USS Dorado SS-248	10/12/1943	U.S. patrol plane near Cuba	78 men lost
USS Corvina SS-226	11/16/1943	Japanese sub, 1st patrol s. Truk	82 men lost
USS Sculpin SS-191	11/19/1943	depth charge and surface guns,	40 men lost 41 pow, 21 s.
USS Capelin SS-289	12/9/1943	unknown 1st patrol	76 men lost
USS Scorpion SS-278	1/5/1944	possible mine 4th patrol East China Sea	77 men lost
USS GrayBack SS-208	2/27/1944	aerial bombs 10th patrol East China Sea	80 men lost
USS Trout SS-202	2/29/1944	depth charged 11th patrol Philippines	79 men lost
USS Tullibee SS-284	3/26/1944	own torpedo 4th patrol	79 men lost 1 survived
USS Gudgeon SS-211	4/18/1944	air/surface 12th patrol off Saipan	80 men lost
USS Herring SS-233	6/1/1944	shore battery, 8th patrol, Matsuwa Is.	80 men lost
USS Golet SS-361	6/14/1944	possible depth charge, 2nd patrol n. of Japan	82 men lost
USS S-28 SS-133	7/4/1944	on training, off Hawaii	50 men lost
USS Robalo SS-273	7/26/1944	3rd patrol off Palawan	84 men lost
USS Flier SS-250	8/13/1944	possible mine, 2nd patrol	80 men lost 8 survived
USS Harder SS-257	8/24/1944	depth charge 6th patrol near Bataan	84 men lost
USS Seawolf SS197	10/3/1944	sunk by USS Rowell DE n. of Moritai 15th	102 men lost
USS Escolar SS-294	10/17/1944	mine, 1st patrol Yellow Sea	82 men lost
USS Darter SS-227	10/24/1944	ran aground Bombay Shoal	no loss of life
USS Shark II SS-314	10/24/1944	depth charged, 3rd patrol off Hainan	90 men lost
USS Tang SS-306	10/24/1944	own torpedo 5th patrol 80 men lost	9 survived
USS Albacore SS-218	11/7/1944	mine 11th patrol, of Hokkaido	80 men lost
USS Growler SS-215	11/8/1944	depth charge, 12th patrol S. China Sea	84 men lost
USS Scamp SS-277	11/11/1944	mine, 8th patrol near Tokyo Bay	83 men lost
USS Swordfish SS-193	1/12/1945	possible mine near Okinawa	83 Men lost
USS Barbel SS-316	2/4/1945	aerial bombs 3rd patrol Palawans	81 men lost
USS Kete SS-369	3/20/1945	Japanese sub, 2nd patrol near Okinawa	87 men lost
USS Trigger SS-237	3/28/1945	aircraft/surface 12th patrol	91 men lost
USS Snook SS279	4/8/1945	possibly sub, 9th patrol near Hainan Is.	88 men
USS Lagarto SS-371	5/3/1945	by mine layer 2nd patrol Gulf of Siam	88 men lost
USS Bonefish SS-223	6/18/1945	depth charged, 8th patrol, near Suzu Misaki	85 men lost
USS Bullhead SS-332	8/6/1945	aircraft depth charge, 3rd patrol Lumbok St.	84 men lost
USS Cochino SS-345	8/26/1949	battery explosion, Norway	lost 7 men from Tusk
USS Stickleback SS-415	5/30/1958	collision w/ USS Silverstein DE-534	no loss of life
USS Thresher SSN-593	4/10/1963	believed piping failure on test dive	112 crew 17 civilians
USS Scorpion SSN-589	5/22/1968	believed battery explosion off Azores	99 men lost

Prologue

The intention of this book is not to be a concise or complete account of the Drum's war record but to bring together in one place as much of the history of her as possible. The war patrol narratives are taken from the actual patrol reports but only the significant sections included with the intention of giving the reader a rough idea of what the war patrols were like, and from records found onboard the Drum in recent years and from talking with the crew members at their annual reunions. I have also used a couple of small incidents about two other boats, the Archerfish and the Barb to illustrate what it was like to be a submarineer. The Drum has appeared in two other books, Final Patrol by Don Keith is an excellent book about all the submarines that made war patrols and are now on display in museums around the country, with brief tales of the improtant patrols and a good reminder of why we need to preserve these boats. The War Below by James Scott is also a good read about the Drum, the Silversides and the Tang. It is focused on the important patrols and on the skippers. The history of the Drum is focused on the boat and the crews from keel laying to present day. At one crew reunion I thanked the crew for bringing the Drum back so I would have something to do in my retirement; they assured me that was not the reason they had in mind at the time.

There are twenty one submarines on display around the country but only nine still in their WWII configuration; some of the others were modified after the war to make them more streamlined for speed and quiet and to be able to stay submerged for longer periods. The others were built after the war for special purposes in some cases and to test new hull designs for the new nuclear power that was coming. There is one nuclear powered submarine on display, the USS Nautilus SS-594, the first one. Each museum submarine is unique in its own way and history and it is important to preserve each one. Several of them are by themselves and are generally in better shape with a couple of exceptions. The boats that are a part of a museum with other ships don't get the care or attention they need. The museums when they got the ships and submarines didn't know how much maintainence it takes to keep these vessels in good condition and by the time the rust is bad enough to draw serious attention it is almost too late and expensive. They weren't considered as historic yet because there were still a lot of the diesel boats operating into the '70s and the patrol reports weren't de-classified until 1974. The Drum is fortunate to have been taken out of the water and put on permanent dry land display in 2001. This is allowing the work to be done by a park employee and myself, a volunteer, and over a long period of time so it is not costing much and the story about the restoration is the third part of this book. The boats that have to go into a dry dock are the ones in trouble, there just isn't enough money. I am also hoping to raise awareness of this problem for all the museums so maybe something can be done before we lose some of our ships and boats. You can go to two web sites to view and find out about the museums in your area. They are www.submarinemuseums.org for the submarines and www.hnsa.org for all of the ships and submarines.

The First Life

New Construction

And

World War II

The Beginning

11 September 1940. After a low temperature of 41 degrees during the night, the day would get up to 71 degrees for the birth of the newest of what was to become the Navy's new Gato class Fleet Submarine, and the start of the long and remarkable history of the USS Drum SS-228 at Portsmouth Navy Shipyard in Portsmouth, New Hampshire. The Drum may have been the seventeenth on the contract list but she became the first started and commissioned (too bad they couldn't have renamed the class). This started the long list of firsts for the Drum:

First Gato keel laid 11 September 1940

First Gato commissioned 1 November 1941

First Gato to sink an enemy ship 2 May 1942

First Gato to be depth charged 2 May 1942

First Gato with Fairbanks-Morse engines The Tambor class that were built at Portsmouth were the first to get these
First submarine to be opened as a museum 4 July 1969

First submarine to have a movie filmed inside for all interior scenes April 2009

It is believed that she is the second submarine in the world to have air conditioning (the USS Chalot may have been first)

Prior to the Gato class the Navy had been experimenting with different classes of submarines to find the right combination of size, speed and armament to fulfill the new role of Fleet Submarine. The Gatos were designed to be able to run with the fleet with higher surface speeds, longer range, to protect the fleet and do reconnassance for the fleet. The Gatos were 311'9" long , 27' wide, surface speed of about 20 knots, submerged speed of about 8-9 knots (for just one hour) 1-2 knots for about 24 hours. They had six torpedo tubes and could carry a total of 24 torpedoes with all tubes loaded, had a 3" deck gun and 20MM machine guns with mounts for .30 cal and later .50 cal. Machine guns. They were to have a patrol endurance of up to sixty days and have more comforts for the crew. The Gato class would become known as thin skin boats because their test depth was 300' (below that the warranty is off) while previous classes were limited to 250' or less (except for three experimental boats which were 300' test depth boats; the USS Argonaut SS166 commssioned 2 April 1928, USS Narwhal SS 167 commssioned 15 May 1930 and the USS Nautilus SS 168 commissioned 1 July 1930), and the followon Balao class could go to 400'.

The Drum would soon be joined with three sisters at Portsmouth Naval Shipyard

USS FlyingFish SS-229 Keel laid 6 December 1940, Launched 9 July 1941, Commissioned 10 December 1941
USS Finback SS-230 Keel laid 5 February 1940, Launched 25 August 1941, Commissioned 31 January 1942
USS Haddock SS-231 Keel laid 31 March 1940, Launched 20 October 1941, Commissioned 14 March 1942

At Electric Boat Shipyard in Groton, Connecticut the following Gatos were in the works.

USS Gato SS-212 Keel laid 5 October 1940, Launched 21 August 1941 Commissioned 31 December 1941
USS Greenling SS-213 Keel laid 12 November 1940, Launched 20 September 1941, Commissioned 21 January 1942
USS Grouper SS-214 Keel laid 28 December 1940, Launched 27 October 1941, Commissioned 12 February 1942
USS Growler SS-215 Keel laid 10 February 1941, Launched 22 November 1941, Commissioned 20 March 1942 Lost 11/8/44 12th patrol
USS Grunion SS-216 Keel laid 1 March 1941, Launched 22 December 1941, Commssioned 11 April 1942 Lost 7/8/42 1st patrol
USS Guardfish SS-217 Keel laid 1 April 1941, Launched 20 January 1942, Commissioned 8 May 1942
USS Albacore SS-218 Keel laid 1 April 1941, Launched 17 February 1942, Commissioned 1 June 1942 Lost 11/7/44 11th patrol

At Mare Island Naval Shipyard in Vallejo, California the following boats were in the works

USS Silversides SS-236 Keel laid 4 November 1940, Launched 26 August 1942, Commissioned 15 December 1941
USS Trigger SS-237 Keel laid 1 February 1941, Launched 22 October 1941, Commissioned 30 January 1942 Lost 3/28/45 12th patrol
Of these first thirteen Gatos, only the Drum and Silversides are left.

Submarines would later be built at Manitowac, Wisconsin and some at Cramp Shipyard in Philidelphia.
A total of 73 Gato class were build by 1943 and they had to carry the war until our fleet could be rebuilt and constructed. For the first two years of the war our submarines sank 73% of all Japanese shipping sunk and for the war they sank 33% of all Japanese Naval ships and 65% of all of their merchant ships. Drum placed eighth for tonnage sunk.

This is the keel being laid from another submarine

This is the upper level of after battery in another submarine; this would be the crews berthing area, note the absence of the wiring and piping yet to be installed. The diameter of the pressure hull is only 16 feet and inside this must be crammed all the equipment, supplies and of course 72-83 crew. Miles of wiring were run through the boat and I can picture the electrician with the end of one wire left to be run and wondering where it goes. The wiring bundles were tied together with small cotton cord. It amazes me how they bent the pipes and wires to go around obstructions and each other. I can't imagine how they got them all connected.

The boats were built in sections about 12 feet long and welded together (the Drum was one of the first all welded submarines) and then holes were cut to add in the equipment and machinery, the piping and wiring run. There would be over a hundred workers all over and in the boat and during the summer months it would be very hot with little to no ventilation and extremely noisy. Shipyards are not fun places to work but very rewarding to see the finished creation.

The launching of the USS Drum SS-228 12 May 1941

In April a few of the crew had arrived, we found invoices for office supplies onboard in 2009.

In October of 1941 the prospective crew of the Drum started to arrive and they lived in barracks at the ship yard and started to learn their new boat and train on it. We found invoices showing where they were having trouble getting cold weather clothing because of the war in Europe and our convoys delivering supplies to England.

In November through February the Drum crew underwent sea trials checking out their new boat, training and getting repairs made. They continued to be plagued with the lack of cold weather clothing and could not get all the repairs made. Pages 5-6 show is the report from their sea trials. Sea trials are very tense, especially the first dives, hoping all the welds and pipes were completed and strong. There would be many things that don't work quite right and have to be fixed. Each time out more of the equipment would be tested and the crew learn how to operate it. On these boats everyone in the crew had to be able to operate every piece of equipment, know every valve and switch and pipe and be able to draw all the systems. There are reports from other boats that when they returned from sea trials they found a piece of duct tape over a hole through the pressure hull and it didn't leak; good tape.

IN REPLY REFER TO

U. S. S. DRUM

February 2, 1942.

MEMORANDUM FOR COMMANDER SUBMARINE DIVISION 101.

There is below a summary of the activities of the DRUM since her acceptance by the Board of Inspection and Survey:-

Jan 5 - Fired gun during forenoon; returned to navy yard during afternoon to fix salt water leak into reduction gear sumps.

Jan 6 - At navy yard repairing leak in gear sumps.

Jan 7 - Conducted training dives.

Jan 8 - Conducted training dives.

Jan 9 - Conducted training dives.

Jan 10- Heavy snowfall prevented operations--returned to navy yard to correct numerous unsatisfactory items. The more important work included: (1) Fresh water cooling system #2 and #3 main engines, (2) Vibration of main motor and reduction gear lubricating liner, (3) Vibration #4 main engine, (4) Adjustments to RADAR, WDA echo-ranging and sound installation, and fathometer, (5) Silver soldering joints of #4 air bank.

Jan 11- At navy yard correcting unsatisfactory items.

Jan 12- At navy yard correcting unsatisfactory items.

Jan 13- At navy yard correcting unsatisfactory items.

Jan 14- At navy yard correcting unsatisfactory items.

Jan 15- Underway 1145; made one running dive.

Jan 16- Conducted full power run, and training dives.

Jan 17- Conducted training dives; returned to navy yard to correct numerous unsatisfactory items. The more important work included: (1) Fresh water cooling systems #2 & #3 main engines, (2) Vibration #4 main engine, (3) Vibration of main motor and reduction gear lubricating piping.

Jan 18- Continued correction of unsatisfactory items.

Jan 19- Conducted training dives; underway during night.

Jan 20- Conducted training dives. During unofficial deep dive serious leak in maneuvering room soft patch developed.

Jan 21- Conducted all day submerged patrol; underway during night.

Jan 22- Conducted all day submerged patrol; ran full power 2 engines during night.

Jan 23- Conducted practice approaches on U.S.S. CHEWINK, made training dives. Underway during night.

Jan 24- Conducted 6 hour battery discharge; returned to navy yard at 1300 to correct numerous unsatisfactory items. The more important work included: (1) Vibration of main motor and reduction gear lubricating piping, (2) Completed silver solder work in #4 air bank, (3) Vibration of #4 main engine, (4) Fresh water cooling system #2 and #3 main engines, (5) Maneuvering room soft patch leak, (6) Install DQ equipment.

- 1 -

IN REPLY REFER TO

U. S. S. DRUM

February 2, 1942.

MEMORANDUM FOR COMMANDER SUBMARINE DIVISION 101.

Jan 25 - Continued work at navy yard.
Jan 26 - Continued work at navy yard.
Jan 27 - Continued work at navy yard.
Jan 28 - Continued work at navy yard.
Jan 29 - Made one dive and sustained casualty to bow plane rigging gear. Returned to yard.
Jan 30 - At navy yard; correcting bow plane rigging gear.
Jan 31 - At anchor lower harbor correcting bow plane rigging gear.
Feb 1 - Conducted deep dive. Made training dives and departed Portsmouth area.

Respectfully,

R. H. RICE,
Lieut.Comdr., U.S. Navy,
Commanding.

Note the serious leak in Maneuvering during a test dive on 20 January. The leak was on what is called a soft patch. This is a plate that covers most of the compartment to allow the removal of the electrical cubicle which controls the ship's propulsion motors underneath it to facilitate the repair of the motors. The leak occurred on their first dive to test depth, 300', and shorted out all electrical in the boat. They got to the surface and back to the shipyard. There was a rush to get the Drum completed because the war had just started and her services was needed. The shipyard didn't have time to drill out all the rivets, pull and reset the patch so they built a drip tray under the seam with drain lines to the bilge. It leaked throught the whole war, especially after a depth charge attack. Most of the other problems didn't get fixed either and the crew had to fight these problems and the enemy.

After all the test dives and what repairs were to be made (many left to be done by the crew or Pearl Harbor), and training, the Drum left PNSY 17 February 1942 under escort to the Panama Canal. On the 18th the crew thought they saw three torpedoes fired at them by a German U-boat but after the war no records of one being in the area could be found. On the 24th a U.S. bomber dropped two bombs at the Drum but missed, we later lost two submarines in this area by U.S. bombers. Passed through the canal on 26 and 27 February and left Balboa on 1 March. The Drum arrived at Pearl on the 16th of March 1942 and underwent four days of up keep and then eight days of torpedo practice. Propeller guards were installed 3/21/42, mine cable cutting gear removed 4/3/42.

The War Patrols
FIRST PATROL

First Patrol

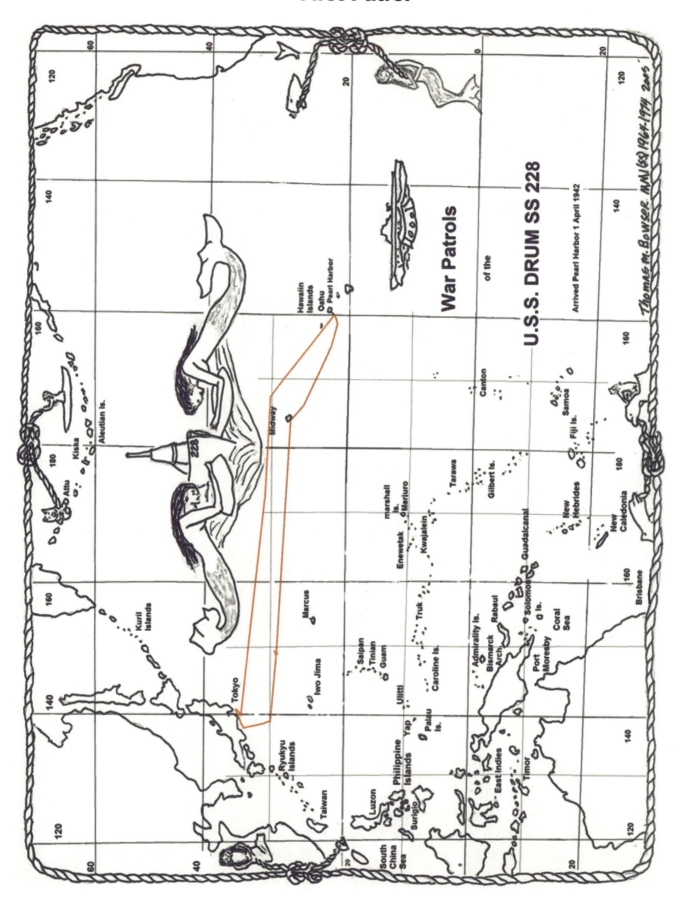

The Drum unloaded all torpedoes and loaded vitamins and medical supplies for Bataan and left on the 6th of April on a secret mission to take the much needed medicines to the Philippines. They got as far as Midway and were turned around because Corregidor was about to fall. They returned to Pearl and on the 15 and 16th off loaded medical supplies and reloaded torpedoes.

The USS Drum fired a total of 133 torpedoes with 38 hits sinking 15 ships according to the Navy, placing it 8th in total tonnage sunk. It received over 300 depth charges.

During the war we would lose 52 submarines, one out of five, with a loss of 3,507 men. Almost half of those were lost on or before their first three patrols. Five were lost to friendly fire, five ran aground on reefs and the crews were rescued, two were lost to their own torpedoes. Aircraft was the biggest threat to the submarines and they quickly learned to surface at night to recharge the batteries, get fresh air and refill the air flasks with compressed air using the air compressors. At times they would go a few days without being able to get a star sight to fix their position and even than the charts of the South Pacific were not very complete.

Patrol 1 Commanding Officer LCdr R.H. Rice

17 April 1942 Left Pearl Harbor
21 April Stopped at Midway for fuel
1 May On station in the approaches to Tokyo Bay, at 2124 spotted a patrol plane close and submerged, surface 2210. At "2355 spotted a medium size ship with large top hamper about two miles on port bow. Swung to close and attack."
2 May At 0002 they fired 2 torpedoes getting one hit (which sank the Sea Plane Tender Mizuho, 9,000 tons) then became aware of a destroyer closing fast, dove and fired one torpedo, missed. In 2009 it was learned that the Mizuho had been converted to carry mini submarines and had ten on board and was part of the task force for the invasion of Midway. The Drum went back to periscope depth and spotted destroyer at 1500 yards fired three torpedoes, all missed, could not train scope due to cable jam cocking the bearing, made repairs and then they underwent a long series of depth charge attacks lasting 16 hours and 31 depth charges were counted. The periscopes were hoisted by wire cable and electric motors until June 1945.
7 May Blew out negative tank flood valve gasket and could not use negative tank to aid in depth control for remainder of patrol. Broached from 90' deep due to heavy seas.
9 May Attack #4 1353 spotted a ship of approximately 5-6000 tons, (loaded and exceptionally neat and new looking) they fired 4 from stern tubes, 1 hit, violent explosion. Sinking a cargo vessel 4,000 tons.
13 May 0928 Submerged 9 miles off Tsumeki Saki light spotted inbound steamer. Attack #5 they fired 1, 1 hit split in two sinking cargo vessel Shonan Maru 5,246 tons. Planes attack and dropped bombs, no hits, depth charged for 1 ½ hours.
16-17 May Master gyro erratic, renewed bearings
19 May Broached from periscope depth off Tokyo Bay, they were spotted and depth charged. Still having gyro problems. Surfaced in strong northwest wind and heavy seas. (Broaching is exposing the periscope shears or sail or worse the whole topside.)
20 May Experienced difficulty getting ship under in heavy seas. Worked on gyro. Riding out storm.
22 May Sighted 6 ships and numerous small vessels, could not close.
25 May 1430 Made approach on small steamer, allowed to pass. 1600 commenced approach on north bound coastal steamer Attack #6 they fired 1, I hit sinking cargo vessel Kitakata Maru 2,300 tons.

28 May Attack #7 they fired 5 at a Naval Tender, all missed, target maneuvered to avoid

1 June Leave station heading back to Pearl Harbor. 5-7 June looking for convoy and damaged ships from battle of Midway, none found.
12 June Arrived Pearl Harbor with Narwhal and Trigger

Note: The periscopes were originally raised and lowered with electric motors and cables and #1 scope was used in the control room which required a periscope depth of 55' while the #2 scope was used in the conning tower and had a use depth of 65'.

17 torpedoes fired – 4 hit   9,000 total miles traveled
 48 depth charges counted

Ships Sunk
2 May Sea Plane Tender Mizuho 9,000 Tons
9 May Cargo Unknown 4,000 Tons
13 May Cargo Shonan Maru 5,246 Tons
25 May Cargo Kitakata Maru 2,300 Tons

The air conditioning was run when submerged and did a good job (the air conditioner kept the boat at a pleasant 90-95 degrees but when it was secured to conserve power or for quite running the boat would get up to 120, the crew mostly wore shorts and sandals and everything was always damp and the deck was covered with condensation). The submarine USS Cachalot SS-170 may have been the first boat to have air conditioning but the Gato class boats were the first to have it in production. On a couple of long submerged periods CO_2 absorbent had to be spread and some oxygen bled into the boat from the O_2 bottles. Food was good and varied with three cooks. The first time they were depth charged the refrigerator compressors were secured for rig for quiet; it was some time before it was noticed the temperature had risen in the refer which resulted in the loss of some meat. It has been rumored that submarines and the crew smelled bad. There was always the odor of diesel fuel and exhaust, hydraulic oil, cooking odors, body odor, toilet odor and of course just about everyone smoked. An illustration of what it was like is the story of the USS Archerfish crew that wanted to bring a skunk on board. When they asked the captain he said "what about the smell?" The crew replied "oh that's ok, he will get used to it- we did". They took the skunk with them and it is reported that the boat smelled better.

Meals were

0330-0430 Breakfasts
1130-1230 Dinners
1930-2030 Suppers

With soup and sandwiches at 1600
Duration of patrol – 57 days, 31 days on station
Rice had a fold up bunk installed in the bridge area so he could nap on the bridge while on the surface. When the plane was spotted on 1 May and the boat dove, Rice didn't have time to get his mattress, it was never found. The bunk was removed in the shipyard period after the 8th patrol.

The first patrol of the Drum and the patrols of other submarines that were already in the war are remarkable in that before the war we thought submarines were defensive weapons and the crews were trained to defend the fleet and do reconnaissance and were meant to stay with the fleet. After the attack on Pearl Harbor there wasn't any fleet left and they were told they had to go out on their own and learn how to be offensive and aggressive. Prior to WWII none of our submarines had been depth charged and they had to learn how to evade and survive these attacks. They also were finding out that the new Mark 14 torpedoes were defective. The torpedoes had a new magnetic exploder that was designed to sense the magnetic field of the steel hulled targets and explode underneath the ships which would break their keel. It never worked. Also the new torpedoes had only been tested with lighter practice warheads and it was found they ran up to 12 feet deeper than set. The contact exploder would not work if the torpedo hit straight on; it would crush before it could set off the detonator. There were also occasional problems with the gyro that controlled the direction and sometimes they would go wherever they wanted, we lost two submarines to their own torpedoes doing a circular run. When the problems were reported to headquarters, the misses were blamed on improper approaches and the other problems were blamed on the crews doing improper maintenance on the torpedoes. It took two years for the problems to be corrected and it was extremely frustrating for the crews. The crew also had to contend with solving and fixing all the problems with the equipment that didn't get repaired during sea trials.

When the Japanese bombed Pearl Harbor they made several major errors. The first being they thought submarines were defensive weapons and they didn't attack the submarines or their repair facilities, the next was they didn't destroy the fuel farm right behind the submarine base and they didn't destroy the dry docks and shipyards. The first Japanese plane shot down was done from the USS Tautog SS-199, a crewman ran up on deck with a machine gun and shot a plane down. They were making their torpedo runs on the battleships right over the submarines.

The Crew for the first patrol

Name	Rank	Role
Rice, Robert H.	LCdr	Captain
Nicholas, Nicholas J.	Lt.	Exec. Officer
Kimmel, Manning M.	Lt.	
Rindskopf, Maurice H.	Ltjg.	
Harper, John D.	Ens.	
Ramsing, Verner U.	Ens.	

Alamia, Anthony J.	F2c (fireman second class)
Anderson, Robert L.	EM3c (electrician mate third class)
Applegate, Elvin C.	TM2c (torpedo man second class)
Armstrong, Kenneth G.	EM1c (electrician mate first class)
Baker, Nesbert D.	AS (able bodied seaman) 5 letters addressed to him were found in the galley In March 2008
Barrell, David C.	EM1c
Bell, Edgar A.	F1c (fireman first class)
Buckbee, William D.	EM2c
Burke, John A.	EM3c
Caverly, John E.	MM2c (machinist mate second class)
Caviness, Daniel D.	RM2c (radio man second class)
Cleveland, Edward C.	MM1c
Conyers, Milton E.	TM2c

Crowe, Audley L.	GM1c (gunners mate first class)
Dalwitz, Wilbert W.	AS
Dozier, Henry M.	MM2c
Dzik, Edward H.	SC2c (store keeper second class)
Eller, Dock M.	MM1c
Ferguson, Donald L.	S1c
Flynn, Thomas Jr.	S2c
Galas, Alexander	SM3c
Ganley, John F. Jr.	MM1c
Getzewich, Julian	MM1c
Gurganus, Arthur A.	CTM
Habermehl, Bernard J.	F1c
Haines, Orval G.	PhM1c (pharmacist mate first class)
Hardin, "E" "M"	AS
Harris, Charles E.	TM2c
Helgerson, Joseph	AS
James, Willie	Matt3c (steward for officers)
Jewell, Conrad D.	TM3c
Kess, Samuel S.	F1c
Krooner, Edward W.	MM2c
LaMark, Christopher P.	S1c
Lang, Emerson C.	F1c
Leach, Gilbert E.	F1c
Lehman, Roland E.	TM2c
Lytle, George W.	Matt1c
Manning, Robert L.	CMM
Martin, Armor W.	F3c
Martin, Sidney J.	QM1c (quartermaster first class)
McKinney, Samuel W.	F2c
McClendon, William H.	SM1c
Morgan, Ernest L.	CEM
Murphy, Arthur C.	EM3c
Otto, Delbert R.	MM1c
Pepper, Ruben H.	CEM
Psencik, Robert L.	MM1c
Pyle, Clarence L.	TM1c
Rich, Jack M.	F2c
Rogers, John D.	EM2c
Rosset, Waldo D.	EM3c
Ryan, Joesph, E.	MM1c
Satterwhite, Marshall	TM2c
Smith, Walter L.	S2c
Sponseller, Howard L.	TM1c
Sullenger, James M.	FC1c
Swarts, Richard	YM1c (yeoman first class-Swarts left his own name off the sailing list)
Vaughan, Donald O.	RM3c
Walsh, Edward F.	SC1c
Wentz, Royce E.	S1c
Whitright, Earl B.	EM3c

Wilkinson, Edward N.	RM1c
Wright, Lowell S.	MM2c
York, Keith L.	S1c

Six Officers and sixty five Enlisted

Fourteen men transferred off after first patrol

Ferguson, Donald L.	S1c
Flynn, Thomas Jr.	S2c
Galas, Alexander	SM3c
Getzewich, Julian	MM1c
Habermehl, Bernard J.	F1c
Hardin, "E" "M"	AS
Harris, Charles E.	TM2c
James, Willie	Matt3c
Jewell, Conrad D.	TM3c
Kess, Samuel S.	F1c
Krooner, Edward W.	MM2c Received Navy Commendation Medal
Morgan, Ernest L.	CEM
Psencik, Robert L.	MM1c
Rogers, John D.	EM2c
Smith, Walter L.	S2c
Swarts, Richard	YM1c

The Navy would transfer some of the crew off of each boat after every patrol. Some would be sent to new construction so the new boats had some qualified experienced crew to train the others and some would be sent to advanced schools for their equipment. The Navy tried to rotate crewman off a boat after 3-4 patrols but the Drum was known as a happy and lucky boat after the second patrol and the crew didn't want to leave. Of the 264 men that served on her during the war patrols, approximately 64 made 8 patrols or more, one doing 12 of the 13 and several doing 11 and 10 patrols. On a few of the patrols the Drum would go to sea with almost half of the crew being new crewman; this was really hard on the crew until they got qualified on a watch station. Normally the watches were 4 hours with 8 off but with so many non-quals they would sometimes have to do 4 and 4. The new seamen would first qualify as lookouts (a very important job) and lookouts were sometimes rotated every 30 minutes depending on the weather. When the boat submerged the lookouts manned the bow and stern planes, another critical position.

SECOND PATROL

Second Patrol

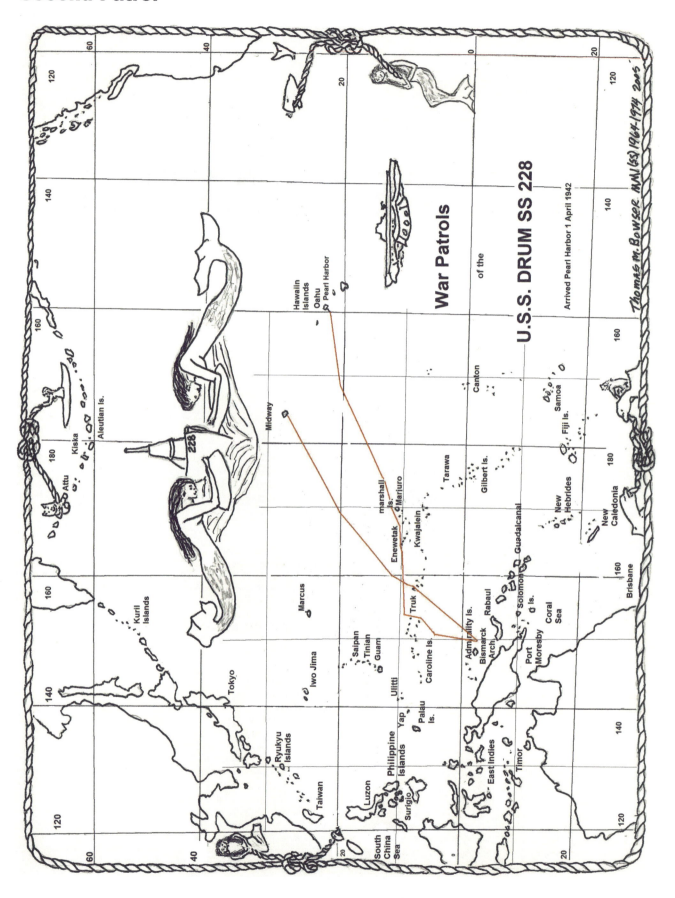

Patrol 2 Commanding Officer Rice

After a refit and resupply in Pearl Harbor lasting about 28 days, Drum left Pearl for patrol in the Caroline and Admiralty Islands.

- 10 July 1942 Left Pearl Harbor Conducted ships drills and crew training.
- 12 July Received orders from CTF-7 to investigate reports of a grounded enemy vessel on Rogelap Atoll.
- 18 July Sighted a grounded ship surrounded by escorts vessels on Rongelap Atoll, could not prosecute attack due to escorts.
- 19 July Blew negative tank flood valve gasket
- 22 July Sighted hospital ship
  Attack 1, sighted cargo fired 2 torpedoes, no hits. Off Ponape, Caroline Is.
- 23 July Gyro problems, repaired gyro
- 27 July found forward torpedo impulse flasks leaking, leaving an air bubble trail. Bled pressure off flasks before diving.
- 30 July-4 August sighted many ships, At 0800 made approach on a 3-400 ton armed cargo vessel standing out of Otta Pass. Lined up for a stern shot but due to limitations of the Mark 15 Torpedoes and radical zig-zags could not get into position to attack. Distant and close depth charges, some close enough to be personnel. (Due to the loss of the supply of torpedoes that were on Corregidor when the Japanese bombed it there was an extreme shortage of torpedoes and the Drum had the stern loaded with Mark 15's which are two feet longer that the 14's and had to be used in the after tubes which are two feet longer than the forward tubes. The Mark 15 is normally carried on surface ships.
- 31 July Received information about an enemy vessel coming out of Rabaul, shifting position to west of Royalist Reef.
- 1 August Sighted two small steamers entering and one leaving Aualap Pass, could not get in position.
- 2 August Sighted more shipping but on the wrong side of the reef. Two Patrol vessels close.
- 3 August Sighted several small craft, maneuvered away and heard explosions near, must have been spotted by aircraft, seas are flat, distant explosions all morning.
- 4-5 August Received information concerning torpedo running depth with different war heads, shifted torpedoes around to try to get some that would run shallower than twenty feet.
- 6 August Attack 2, sighted cargo, fired 3 Mark fifteen torpedoes from stern tubes, no hits, aircraft attacked with bombs. Repack port Propeller shaft stern tube.
- 11 August Spotted Japanese I class submarine in heavy rain, could not attack.
- 15 August Spotted enemy vessel, made approach but could not attack due to circling aircraft.
- 17 August Off Kavieng, Admiralty Islands. Attack 3, fired 3 torpedoes at destroyer, no hits. Depth charged some close, minor damage, radio antenna lead in wires leaking, main engine exhaust valves leaking.
- 24 August End of patrol headed home to Midway
- 2 Sept Arrive Midway

8 Torpedoes fired, possible 1 hit
8500 miles to and from station

Duration of patrol – 55 days on station 36 days

Problems with #1 lighting motor/generator and the pitometer log (measures speed and distance). Main engine exhaust valves leaking

The Drum had two periscopes, #1 was used in the control room which required a shallower periscope depth of 55', #2 was used in the conning tower and had a periscope depth of 65', this was the preferred scope, they were raised and lowered with electric motors and cables which caused some problems. During this patrol #2 scope fogged up and couldn't be used The crew raised #1 to the control room, blocked it in position, than shifted the cables from #2 to #1 and raised it the rest of the way into the conning tower. The periscopes at this time had very small optics and weren't of much use at night.

The Crew for the second patrol 1 new officer and 15 new enlisted men

Rice, Robert H.	LCdr	Captain
Nicholas, Nicholas J.	Lt.	Exec. Officer
Kimmel, Manning M.	Lt.	
Rindskopf, Maurice H.	Lt.	
Harper, John D.	Ltjg.	
Ramsing Verner U.	Ens.	
Pridonoff, Eugene	Ens	

Alamia, Anthony J.	F2c
Anderson, Gilbert M.	S2c
Anderson, Robert L.	EM3c
Applegate, Elvin C.	TM2c
Armstrong, Kenneth G.	EM1c
Baker, Nesbert D.	S2c
Barrell, David C.	EM1c
Bell, Edgar A.	MM2c
Buckbee, William D.	MM2c
Bundy, John T.	MM2c
Burke, John A.	EM3c
Carmean, Myrlon H.	S2c
Caverly, John E.	MM2c
Chase, Carl C. Jr.	Sc2
Cleveland, Edward C.	MM1c
Conyers, Milton E.	TM2c
Chriswell, Lane P.	YM1c
Crowe, Audley L.	GM1c
Dalwitz, Wilbert W.	S2c
Dawson, Elijah Jr.	Matt2c
Deighan, Walter F.	S2c
Dozier, Henry M.	MM2c
Dzik, Edward H.	SC2c
Eller, Dock M.	MM1c
Ganley, John F. Jr.	MM1c
Gurganus, Arthur A.	CTM
Haines, Orval G.	CPhM
Helgerson, Joseph	S2c
Kash, Arthur	AS
LaMark, Christopher P.	S1c

Lang, Emerson C.	F1c
Leach, Gilbert E.	F1c
Lehman, Roland E.	TM2c
Lindsay, Robert G. Jr.	RM3c
Lytle, George W.	Matt1c
Martin, Armor W.	F3c
Martin, Sidney J.	QM1c
McKinney, Samuel W.	F2c
McClendon, William H.	SM1c
Murphy, Arthur C.	EM3c
Otto, Delbert R.	MM1c
Pepper, Ruben H.	CEM
Peterson, William J.	AS
Pyle, Clarence L.	TM1c
Reed, Gordon M.	AS
Rich, Jack M.	F1c
Rosset, Waldo D.	EM3c
Ryan, Joesph, E.	MM1c
Satterwhite, Marshall	TM2c
Simko, Frank M.	AS
Simmons, Charles G. Jr.	S2c
Simpson, Clyde R.	AS
Sponseller, Howard L.	TM1c
Stafford, Archie D.	S1c
Szymanski, Ted	AS
Sullenger, James M.	FC1c
Vaughan, Donald O.	RM2c
Vaughan, Richard H.	S2c
Wadja, Steve J.	F3c
Walsh, Edward F.	SC1c
Wentz, Royce E.	S1c
White, Robert E.	F3c
Whitright, Earl B.	EM3c
Wilkinson, Edward N.	RM1c
Wright, Lowell S.	MM2c
York, Keith L.	S1c

Seven Officers and sixty six Enlisted

Nineteen men transferred off after second Patrol

Nicholas, Nicholas J.	Lt.	Exec. Officer

Bundy, John T.	MM2c	
Deighan, Walter F.	S2c	
Ganley, John F. Jr.	MM1c	
Lang, Emerson C.	F1c	Received Navy Commendation Medal

Lehman, Roland E.	TM2c	
Lindsay, Robert G. Jr.	RM3c	
Manning, Robert L.	CMM	
Murphy, Arthur C.	EM3c	
Reed, Gordon M.	AS	
Simko, Frank M.	AS	received Navy/Marine Commendation Medal
Simpson, Clyde R.	AS	
Sponseller, Howard L.	TM1c	received Bronze Star
Stafford, Archie D.	S1c	
Vaughan, Richard H.	S2c	
Walsh, Edward F.	SC1c	
Wilkinson, Edward N.	RM1c	
Wright, Lowell S.	MM2c	
York, Keith L.	S1c	

After each patrol the crew would turn over the boat to a relief crew who would make the repairs and do what maintenance was required. The crew would be on a period of R & R (rest and relaxation) during the refit. While the boats operated out of Pearl Harbor they were put up in the Royal Hawaiian Hotel and were pretty much allowed the freedom to do as they pleased. The refits would last anywhere from two weeks to two months depending on what repairs were needed. When they operated out of Australia, Majuro, Guam and Saipan there were rest camps for the crews with beer supplied. Volley ball, baseball and horse shoes were the favored activities. At the forward islands a sub tender would be stationed there to do the repair work. The tenders had complete machine shops, foundries and any other kind of repair shop. The crew would often have to repair the repairs the tender made when they got under way. The crew would come back on board a week or so before going back to the war, they loaded food and supplies (everyone in the crew, food was stored everywhere. Ammunition for the deck guns, (stored under the galley, the cook was very careful with his ovens) torpedoes, fuel, oil and water. Then they would go to sea for training and to test everything for a few days.

Early in the War there were reports the Mark 14 Torpedoes wouldn't run as far as they were supposed to. The Mk14's were steam powered and burn 100% grain alcohol, they found out the crew was drinking the fuel (we found invoices for lots of pineapple juice and grapefruit juice and thought it was for the vitamins). The Navy put oil and a coloring in the fuel but it didn't take long before stills were made and the crew discovered they could filter it through two loaves of bread. The skippers finally told the crew to leave enough so each torpedo would have a range of 1500 yards, they would just get closer. It turns out this also increased their accuracy.

THIRD PATROL

Third Patrol

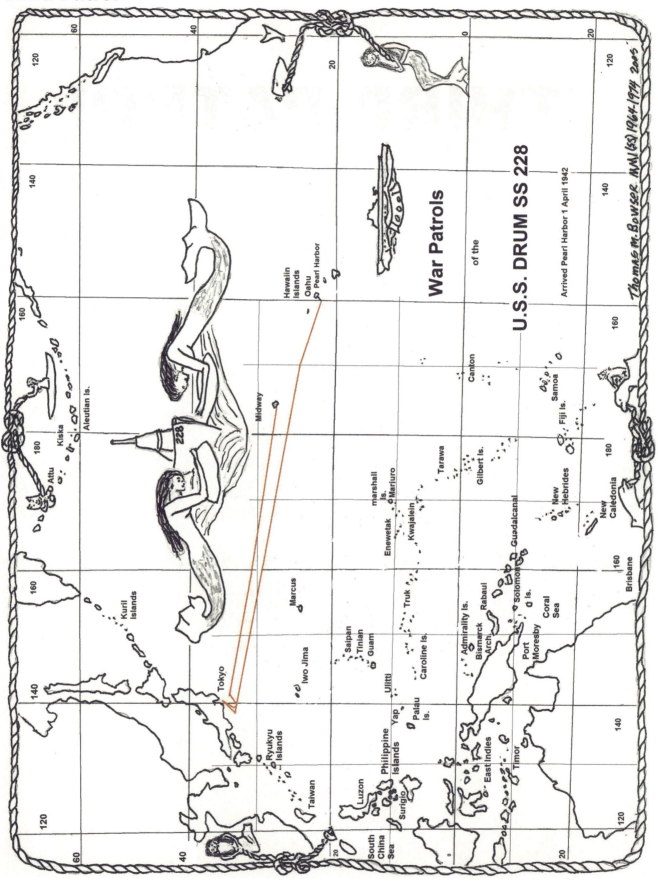

During refit at Midway between patrols 2 & 3 the propeller guards were removed and the fairwater was modified to cut down the silhouette. Port propeller shaft was repacked.
Refit lasted about 21 days.

Patrol 3 Commanding Officer Rice

23 September 1942 Left Midway, experienced overheating on port shaft seals, 24-29 repacked shaft four times.
2 October On station south of Tokyo Bay
3 October Seas rough, cannot maintain depth control at periscope depth.
4 October Sighted cargo, unable to close
7 October Sighted hospital ship
8 October Attack 1, sighted air escorted convoy of four ships, one was trailing about a mile and a half, fired 2 torpedoes at lead cargo, no hits, Fired 2 at second ship, 1 hit, fired 2 at third ship, no hits, attacked by aircraft.
9 October Attempted approach on a target but was too close to daylight and patrol boats and aircraft in area, heavy rain until 1625. Attack 2, 1628 sighted cargo, Fired 2 torpedoes from 1200 yards, 1 premature 1 miss, target turned and opened fire with a deck gun fired 1, 1 hit, ship sank
10-11 Oct Heavy seas no depth control
13 October 1435 Sighted a destroyer to seaward and attempted approach, could not get closer than 5,000 yards, turned back towards coast, spotted convoy of four ships close to shore could not close. 1650 sighted another ship Attack 3, sighted cargo, fired 2 torpedoes, 1 premature, 1 miss, bombed and depth charged
16-18 Oct Heavy seas 1630 on 18th finally determined position.
19 Oct Sighted convoy of six ships and numerous trawlers close in shore, made approach but discovered ships were on other side of what appeared to be fishing nets, cancelled approach so as not to foul nets.
20 October 1545 Sighted three ship convoy with air escorts, started approach. Attack 4 1619, fired 2 torpedoes from stern tubes, 1 hit and ship settled and sank fast, fired 2 at second ship, ship turn as torpedoes were fired, no hits, bombed and depth charged.
22 Oct Just before dawn a surfaced submarine was spotted at 2500 yards, Drum was 3 ½ miles south of its area and figured it was friendly, turned north and cleared area.
25 October Sighted several distant targets, could not get close. Attack 5, sighted cargo at range Of 1250 yards, fired 2 torpedoes, no hits, fired 2 more, 1 premature, no hits
27 October Attack 6, Fired 2 torpedoes, no hits, fired 2 torpedoes, 1 hit, dived to avoid collision with cargo ship.
28 October Left station, heading for Pearl Harbor
8 November Arrived Pearl Harbor

23 torpedoes fired, 4 hits Almost all of the misses were seen to run under the targets.

2290 miles from Midway to station
3580 miles from station to Pearl Harbor

8 October sank passenger/cargo Hague Maru 5,641 Tons
9 October sank cargo Hachimanzan Maru 2,461 Tons
20 October sank cargo Ryunan Maru 5,106 Tons

Duration of patrol 47 days, on station 25 days, Patrol ended early due to expending all but 1 torpedo

The Crew for the third patrol 1 new officer, and 18 new enlisted men

Rice, Robert H.	LCdr Captain
Kimmel, Manning M.	Lt Exec
Rindskopf, Maurice H.	Lt.
Harper, John D.	Ltjg
Dye, Ira	Ltjg.
Ramsing, Verner U.	Ens.
Pridonoff, Eugene	Ens
Alamia, Anthony J.	F2c
Anderson, Gilbert M.	S2c
Anderson, Robert L.	EM2c
Applegate, Elvin C.	TM2c
Armstrong, Kenneth G.	EM1c
Baker, Nesbert D.	S2c
Barrell, David C.	EM1c
Bell, Edgar A.	MM2c
Bourland, James H.	AS
Buckbee, William D.	MM2c
Burke, John A.	EM3c
Carmean, Myrlon H.	S2c
Caverly, John E.	MM2c
Cavines, Daniel D.	RM2c
Chase, Carl C. jr.	Sc2
Caviness, Daniel D.	RM2c
Cleveland, Edward C.	MM1c
Conyers, Milton E.	TM2c
Chriswell, Lane P.	YM1c
Crowe, Audley L.	GM1c
Dalwitz, Wilbert W.	S2c
Dawson, Elijah jr.	Matt2c
Dozier, Henry M.	MM2c
Dzik, Edward H.	SC2c
Eller, Dock M.	MM1c
Gurganus, Arthur A.	CTM
Haines, Orval G.	CPhM
Harris, Charles E.	TM1c
Havens, Paul G.	SC1c
Helgerson, Joseph	S2c
Kash, Arthur	AS
Kess, Samuel S.	F1c
Krooner, Edward W.	MoMM2c
Kuhn, Marvin G.	S2c
LaMark, Christopher P.	S1c
Leach, Gilbert E.	F1c
Lytle, George W.	Matt1c
Martin, Armor W.	F3c

Martin, Sidney J.	QM1c
McKinney, Samuel W.	F2c
McClendon, William H.	SM1c
Nichols, Harvey E.	Sc2
Otto, Delbert R.	MM1c
Parker, Charles W.	S1c
Pepper, Ruben H.	CEM
Peterson, William J.	AS
Pettigrew, Rex L.	F3c
Psencik, Robert L.	MM1c
Pyle, Clarence L.	TM1c
Rich, Jack M.	F1c
Ritchie, Robert W.	F1c
Rosset, Waldo D.	EM3c
Ryan, Joesph, E.	MM1c
Satterwhite, Marshall	TM2c
Savage, Carl H.	S1c
Schaedler, George A.	EM1c
Simmons, Charles G. Jr.	S2c
Stockton, Charles E.	TM3c
Style, Norman V.	RM3c
Szymanski, Ted	AS
Sullenger, James M.	FC1c
Truxton, Joseph J.	F3c
Vaughan, Donald O.	RM2c
Wadja, Steve J.	F3c
Waycasey, William E.	MoMM2c
Wentz, Royce E.	S1c
West, Thomas H.	S2c
White, Robert E.	F3c
Whitright, Earl B.	EM3c
Williamson, Phillip L.	S1c
Wolf, William H.	S2c

Seven Officers and seventy Enlisted

Twenty men transferred off after third patrol

Rice, Robert H.	LCdr	Received Navy Cross
Barrell, David C.	EM1c	
Bourland, James H.	AS	
Caverly, John E.	MM2c	
Cavines, Daniel D.	RM2c	
Chase, Carl C. Jr.	Sc2	
Caviness, Daniel D.	RM2c	
Cleveland, Edward C.	MM1c	
Conyers, Milton E.	TM2c	
Chriswell, Lane P.	YM1c	

Dalwitz, Wilbert W.	AS
Dzik, Edward H.	SC2c
Gurganus, Arthur A.	CTM
Harris, Charles E.	TM1c
McClendon, William H.	SM1c
Pepper, Ruben H.	CEM received Silver Star
Psencik, Robert L.	MM1c
Savage, Carl H.	S1c
Simmons, Charles G. Jr.	S2c

FOURTH PATROL

Fourth Patrol

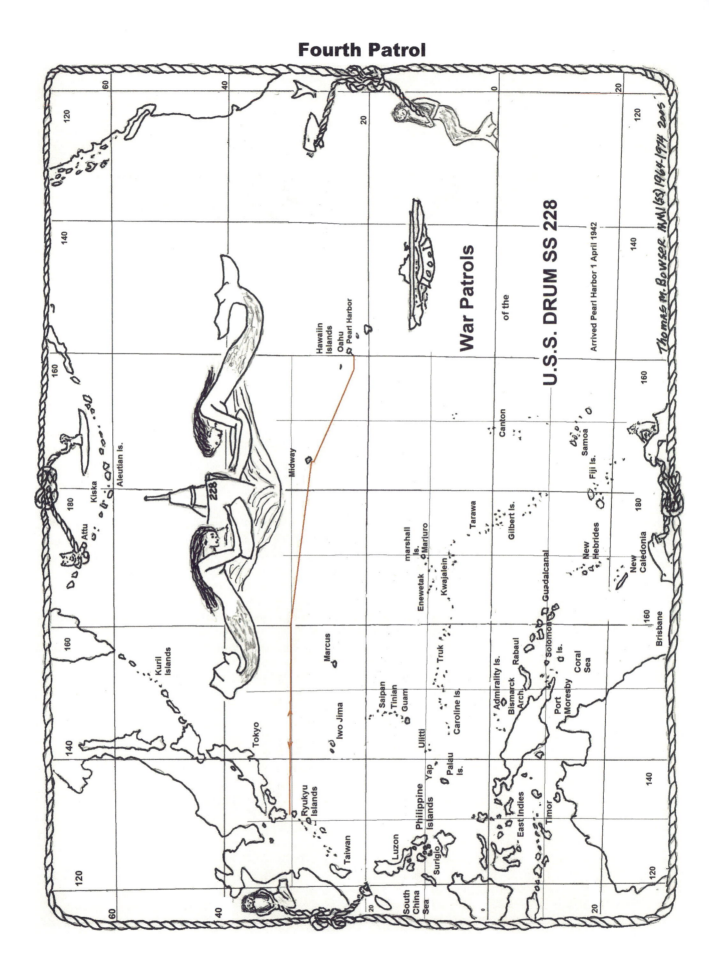

30

During the 21 day refit at Pearl Harbor, the Drum received the SJ and SD radars. LCdr Rice was relieved by LCdr McMahon

Patrol 4 Commanding Officer LCdr B.F. McMahon

29 November 1942 Left Pearl Harbor Conducted ships drills and crew training. Due to shortage of torpedoes, the Drum left on her fourth patrol with only sixteen torpedoes and a load of mines to be planted in the Bungo Suido Straights

3 December Stopped Midway island for fuel and food and to repair SJ radar

12 December 0910 On the surface the SD radar picked up an aircraft 16 miles off, Drum submerged. 0945 Drum surfaced, 1010 lookout spotted smoke on horizon approximately 300 miles southeast of Tokyo. 1020 Sighted aircraft carrier Attack #1 1025 submerged, lost power port shaft temporarily, 1110 fired 4 torpedoes at range of 1200 yards, turned to bring stern tubes into action, heard 2 hits, poppet valves on torpedo tubes leaking taking on water, lost power to port shaft, losing depth control, destroyer approaching, ordered depth 200', 1121 9 close depth charges, 1135 7 close depth charges, boat heavy reaches 350' (50' past test depth) before stopping descent by putting air into safety tank, destroyer still above, 1300 regained port shaft and depth control, destroyer gone. The aircraft carrier was later identified as the escort carrier Ryuho and was only damaged. This was a hard luck ship, it had a 500# bomb dropped on it in April during the Doolittle raid and when the Drum hit it, it was on its first voyage. Later in the war it was leaving Tokyo again and another submarine torpedoed it, again only doing damage, it was tied up in shipyards most of the war.

13 December Working on port shaft interlock.

16 December Arrived on station 1915 surfaced 2120 made SJ radar contact and sighted destroyer which turned on search light, submerged, depth charged

17 December Planted 24 mines in the Bungo Suido south of Japans main island.

21 December Sighted by destroyer which sent blinking light signals, no one onboard understood Japanese so they just blinked something back, the destroyer moved off a bit but came back Sending more signals, the Drum answered back like an apprentice signalman and the destroyer left.

24 December Having trouble receiving messages from headquarters, first Christmas at sea off Japan.

26-31 December Sighted many contacts, could not close

5 January 1943 On the surface, 2245 SJ radar picked up contact range 15,000 yards, commenced closing and approach. Contact is a large merchant ship with two escorts. Attack #2 2320 range 2,000 yards, fired 3 torpedoes at cargo ship off Bungo Suido turned and submerged. 1 hit, depth charged

6 January Just prior to surfacing heard two loud explosions and sound picked up two high speed screws, did not surface until 0250 and cleared area.

8 January Left area on return track.

12 January In heavy seas the shear pins on the bow planes broke, when possible the boat surfaced and replaced pins twice, however the planes were 10 degrees out of alignment which required the planes to be rigged in and out by hand for the remainder of the patrol.

13 January 0755 Sighted smoke on horizon started closing at high speed. 0815 submerged Attack #3 Seas too rough to make periscope attack with problems with bow planes, attack commenced by sound only, fired two torpedoes from depth of 100 feet, heard two hits heard destroyer, stayed submerged until night.

19 January Stopped Midway for fuel

24 January Arrived Pearl Harbor

9 torpedoes fired 2 hits

10,620 miles to and from patrol area

Other problems were a pin on the port motor control lever came out, was easily replaced, problems with a battery bank contactor tripping out, and #3 main engine exhaust valve leaking, Port reduction gear lube oil cooler leak allowing salt water into lube oil, SJ radar training motor overheating-caused by motor and shaft not aligned properly when installed, attack periscope fogging. Seas were rough affecting depth control and skies overcast at least 40% of the time making navigation difficult.

Duration of patrol – 57 days, on station 33 days, Note that attacks were made enroute to and from station.

The Crew for the fourth patrol 2 new officers, including Commanding officer, and 18 new enlisted men

Captain		
McMahon, Bernard F.	LCdr	Captain
Nicholas, Nicholas J	LCdr	Exec.
Kimmel, Manning M.	Lt.	
Rindskopf, Maurice H.	Lt.	
Harper, John D.	Ltjg	
Dye, Ira	Ltjg.	
Ramsing Verner U.	Ens.	
Pridonoff, Eugene	Ens	
Kelly R. O.	Ens.	
Alamia, Anthony J.	F1c	
Anderson, Gilbert M.	F2c	
Anderson, Robert L.	EM2c	
Applegate, Elvin C.	TM2c	
Armstrong, Kenneth G.	EM1c	
Baker, Nesbert D.	SC3c	
Bell, Edgar A.	MoMM2c	
Buckbee, William D.	MoMM1c	
Bundy, John T.	MoMM2c	
Burke, John A.	EM3c	
Carr, Roy Jr.	TM3c	
Carmean, Myrlon H.	S1c	
Crowe, Audley L.	GM1c	
Dawson, Elijah Jr.	Matt1c	
DeGrazio, Tony	CSM	
Dial, Harrel	RT2c	
Dozier, Henry M.	MoMM2c	
Eller, Dock M.	MoMM1c	
Eubanks, James W.	F3c	
Fedor, Robert C.	F3c	

Galas, Alexander	SM3c	
Haines, Orval G.	CPhM	
Havens, Paul G.	SC2c	
Helgerson, Joseph	S2c	
Heller, Jack E.	EM1c	
Ireland, Joe N.	RM2c	
Kane, Thomas P.	S2c	
Kash, Arthur	S2c	
Kearns, Glenn E.	S2c	
Kess, Samuel S.	F1c	
Krooner, Edward W.	MoMM2c	
Kuhn, Marvin G.	S2c	
Leach, Gilbert E.	MoMM2c	
Lindsay, Robert G Jr.	RM3c	
Lytle, George W.	OFck3c	
Martin, Armor W.	F2c	
Martin, Sidney J.	QM1c	
McFadden, Jack L.	F3c	
McKinney, Samuel W.	F1c	
Nichols, Harvey E.	Sc2	
Olson, Robert L.	YM2c	Transferred off 3 Dec at Midway Back on 19 Jan
Otto, Delbert R.	MoMM1c	
Parker, Charles W.	S1c	
Peterson, William J.	S2c	
Pettigrew, Rex L.	F2c	
Pyle, Clarence L.	TM1c	
Rich, Jack M.	F1c	
Ritchie, Robert W.	F1c	
Rosset, Waldo D.	EM3c	
Ryan, Joesph, E.	MoMM1c	
Satterwhite, Marshall	TM2c	
Schaedler, George A.	EM1c	
Simko, Frank M.	F3c	
Stilson, Louis A.	F3c	
Stockton, Charles E.	TM3c	
Stover, Rual C.	S2c	
Style, Norman V.	RM3c	
Sullenger, James M.	FC1c	
Szymanski, Ted	AS	
Truxton, Joseph J.	F3c	
Vaughan, Donald O.	RM1c	
Wadja, Steve J.	F2c	
Waycasey, William E.	MoMM2c	
Wentz, Royce E.	GM3c	
West, Thomas H.	S2c	
White, Robert E.	F2c	
Whitright, Earl B.	EM3c	
Williamson, Phillip L.	S1c	
Wolf, William H.	S2c	
Workman, Thomas M.	TM2c	

Seven Officers and seventy Enlisted

Fifteen men transferred off after fourth patrol

Nicholas, Nicholas J	LCdr Exec.	Awarded Silver Star Star-Navy Commendation Medal
Kimmel, Manning M.	Lt.	Awarded Silver Star-Navy Commendation Medal-Transferred To Robalo which was lost on patrol
Dye, Ira	Ltjg.	Awarded Navy/Marine Medal
Buckbee, William D.	EM2c	
Dial, Harrel	RT2c	
Kess, Samuel S.	F1c	
LaMark, Christopher P.	S1c	
Olson, Robert L.	YM2c	
Otto, Delbert R.	MM1c	Awarded Silver Star
Rosset, Waldo D.	EM3c	
Satterwhite, Marshall	TM2c	
Stilson, Louis A.	F3c	
Truxton, Joseph J.	F3c	
Waycasey, William E.	MoMM2c	
West, Thomas H.	S2c	

FIFTH PATROL

Fifth Patrol

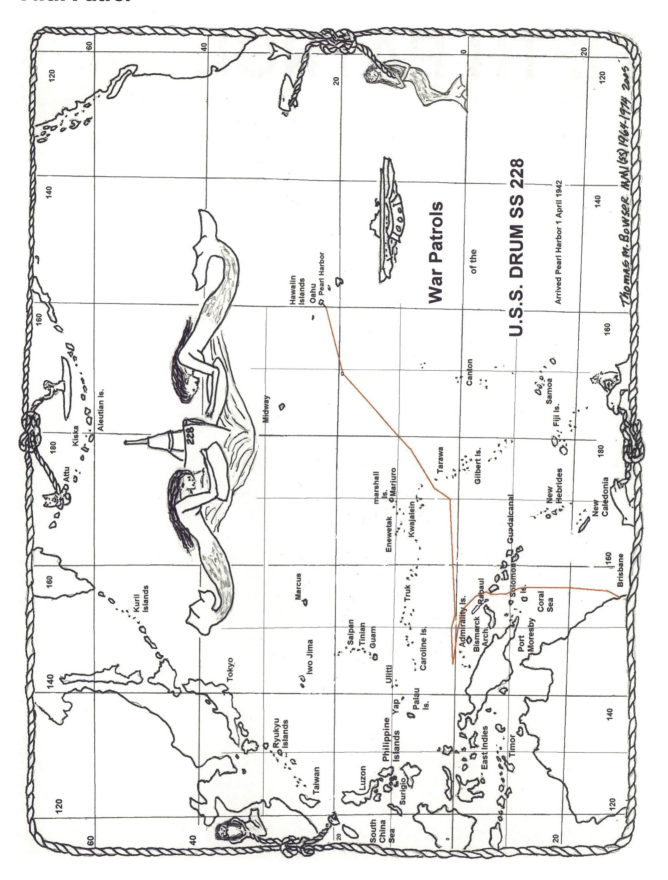

During the almost two month refit between patrols 4 & 5 the fairwater was again modified, the 3" gun aft of the fairwater was removed and a 4" was installed forward of the fairwater, a second 20 mm was installed and most important an ice cream machine and ice cuber were installed. Trim and Drain pumps silenced.

Patrol 5 Commanding Officer McMahon
24 March 1943 Left Pearl Harbor
26 March Stopped Johnston Island Moored to USS Midway for five hours, for fuel and stores and each member of the crew was given one beer.
31 March Repack port shaft seal, test fired 4" and 20mm.
1 April Commenced submerged patrol between Makin and Mathews Islands.
3 April Took photographs of Nauru Island from 1 mile west, in the Gilbert Islands, no military targets sighted. The USS Alabama later conducted shore bombardment of Nauru.
8 April On station off the Admiralty Islands. Received message of a convoy and headed towards its location.
9 April 1158 Sighted smoke at 12,000 yards commenced approach. Attack #1 Convoy consists of four merchant ships and one patrol craft. 1356 fired 3 torpedoes at cargo, went to 200' and commenced evasive maneuvers, 1 hit, depth charged. 1642 surfaced and headed to area of attack spotted lots of debris and retrieved a life ring from Oyama Maru-Tokyo. 1750 started after convoy and at 2115 picked it up on radar at 18,200 yards.
10 April At 0250 Fired three torpedoes range 2800 yards, cleared area to south. Heard two explosions. Commenced trying to get into position for day time attack, 0630 submerged, tracking convoy, 1605 surfaced, no contact with convoy.
14 April 0614-2010 Depth charged while trying to get in position on convoy, spotted patrol plane, submerged, later surfaced, tried to find convoy, broke off due to another friendly submarine in area.
18 April 1214 Sighted smoke, commenced approach on fully loaded freighter. 1346 Attack #3 fired 4 torpedoes, 1 premature 2 hit, swung to bring stern tubes into action, fired 2 at second cargo, 2 premature, fired 2 more, 2 missed. 1430 cleared area. 2010 surfaced lost power port shaft.
22 April Sighted Patrol boat at 0702.
23 April 1156 Sighted smoke 10 miles distance, attempted to track submerged. 1335 Surfaced commenced 4 engine speed run to try to find contact. 1342 sighted smoke again, a single ship. 1422 L. H. Johnson spotted patrol plane, submerged to 150'. 1930 surfaced and commenced pursuit.
24 April 0625 Submerged no sight of contact, 0730 spotted plane through periscope.
25 April- 1 May patrolling Palau, Rabaul and Truk Wewak lanes, weather squally, overcast and poor visibility.
7 May 1925 Surfaced in heavy seas, took water down the hatch flooding the pump room and grounding out most of the equipment in the pump room. All machinery back on line by 0400
8 May Pump room equipment repairs completed.
!0 May Received end of patrol message. Headed for Australia
13 May Arrived in Brisbane, Australia.

12 Torpedoes fired, 5 hits

8341 miles 3598 to station 2836 on station 1903 from station to Brisbane

9 April sank cargo ship Oyama Maru 3,809 Tons
18 April sank cargo ship Nisshun Maru 6,380 Tons

Problems: Port motor field interlock failed for the third consecutive patrol, #4 main engine exhaust valve strainer plate came loose, preventing valve from closing, strainer plates removed. SD radar did not perform well, SJ worked great until attack on 9 April; from then on it was erratic. Noticed excessive smoke from many of the torpedoes, not good in the calm seas of the Solomon Islands area.
Despite the warm weather the boat was comfortable, CO_2 absorbent was spread each morning on diving.

The food obtained from the tender Sperry was not as high a quality as previously. Coca-Cola syrup and hundreds of CO_2 capsules were enjoyed by all hands.

Duration of patrol 51 days, on station 27 days

The Crew for the fifth patrol 2 new officers, including Commanding officer and 15 new enlisted men

Captain	
McMahon, Bernard F.	LCdr Captain
Rindskopf, Maurice H.	Lt. Exec
Harper, John D.	Lt
Ramsing Verner U.	Ltjg.
Pridonoff, Eugene	Ltjg
Hazapis, T.	Ens.
Kelly R. O.	Ens.
Alamia, Anthony J.	MoMM2c
Anderson, Gilbert M.	EM3c
Anderson, Robert L.	EM2c
Applegate, Elvin C.	TM1c
Armstrong, Kenneth G.	CEM
Baker, Nesbert D.	SC3c
Bell, Edgar A.	MoMM2c
Brownwell, Ralph E.	MoMM2c
Bundy, John T.	MoMM1c
Burke, John A.	EM2c
Carr, Roy Jr.	TM3c
Carmean, Myrlon H.	TM3c
Crowe, Audley L.	CGM
Dalwitz, Wailbert, W.	F1c
Dawson, Elijah Jr.	Matt1c
Decoo, George F.	YM1c
DeGrazio, Tony	CSM
Dozier, Henry M.	MoMM1c
Eksterowicz, Edward	F2c
Eller, Dock M.	CMoMM
Eubanks, James W.	F3c
Fedor, Robert C.	EM3c
Fox, Conrad L.	EM3c
Galas, Alexander	SM2c

Haines, Orval G.	CPhM
Havens, Paul G.	SC1c
Helgerson, Joseph	S1c
Heller, Jack E.	EM1c
Ireland, Joe N.	RM2c
Johnson, Leonard M.	S1c
Kane, Thomas P.	S2c
Kash, Arthur	S1c
Kearns, Glenn E.	S2c
Krooner, Edward W.	MoMM1c
Kuhn, Marvin G.	S1c
Lang, Emerson	MoMM1c
Leach, Gilbert E.	MoMM2c
Lindsay, Robert G Jr.	RM3c
Lytle, George W.	OFck2c
McKinney, Samuel W.	F1c
Nichols, Harvey E.	Sc2
Parker, Charles W.	S1c
Peterson, William J.	S1c
Pettigrew, Rex L.	F1c
Phillips, Rollie P.	S1c
Pyle, Clarence L.	TM1c
Reed, Gordon M.	S2c
Rich, Jack M.	MoMM2c
Ritchie, Robert W.	F1c
Rowe, James E.	S2c
Ruebush, Calvin P.	S1c
Ryan, Joesph, E.	MoMM1c
Schaedler, George A.	EM1c
Simko, Frank M.	F2c
Smith, Alvah P.	EM3c
Stockton, Charles E.	TM3c
Stover, Rual C.	S2c
Style, Norman V.	RM3c
Sullenger, James M.	FC1c
Szymanski, Ted	S1c
Vaughan, Donald O.	RM1c
Wadja, Steve J.	F3c
Watson, James D.	SM2c
Wentz, Royce E.	GM3c
White, Robert E.	F1c
Whitright, Earl B.	EM2c
Williamson, Phillip L.	S1c
Wolf, William H.	S2c
Workman, Thomas M.	TM2c
Wright, Lowell S.	MoMM1c

Seven Officers and Seventy Enlisted

Twenty two men transferred off after fifth patrol

Kelly, R. O.   Ens.

Anderson, Gilbert M.	S2c	
Bundy, John T.	MoMM2c	
Dawson, Elijah jr.	Matt2c	
Haines, Orval G.	PhM1c	Silver Star
Havens, Paul G.	SC1c	
Johnson, Leonard M.	S1c	
Kash, Arthur	AS	May have made 6th patrol but not shown on crew list
Kuhn, Marvin G.	S2c	
Lindsay, Robert G Jr.	RM3c	
McKinney, Samuel W.	F1c	
Martin, Armor W.	F3c	
Martin, Sidney J.	QM1c	
Nichols, Harvey E.	Sc2	
Parker, Charles W.	S1c	
Peterson, William J.	AS	
Ryan, Joesph, E.	MM1c	Navy/Marine Medal
Stockton, Charles E.	TM3c	
Wadja, Steve J.	F3c	Navy/Marine Medal
Williamson, Phillip L.	S1c	
Wolf, William H.	S2c	
Wright, Lowell S.	MoMM1c	

SIXTH PATROL

Sixth Patrol

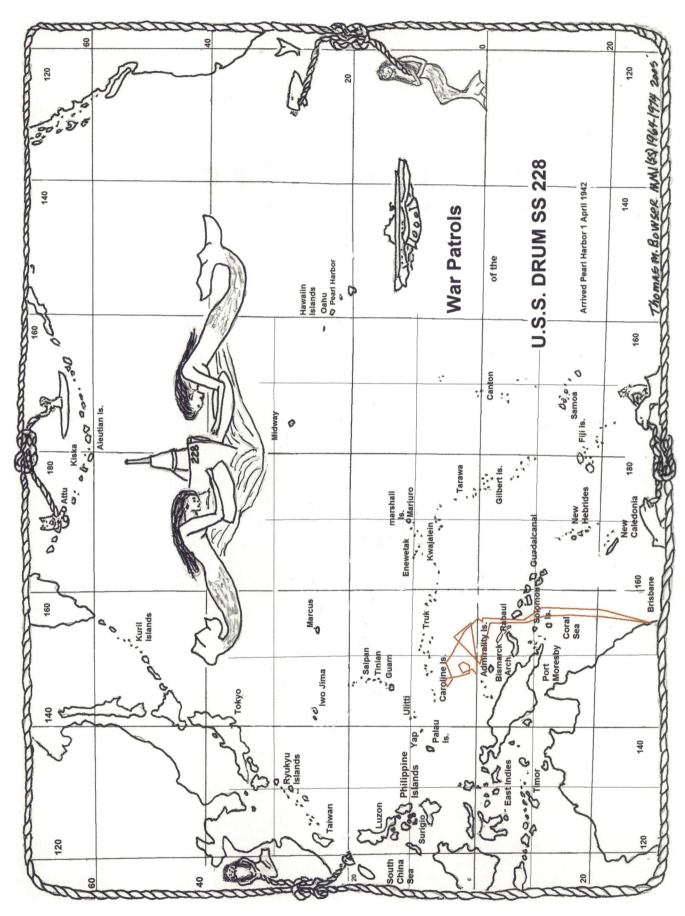

During the normal 3 week refit a bathythermograph was installed to measure sea water temperature at all depths to allow the boat to find a thermal layer to hide under. 3"/50 deck gun removed and a 4"/50 was put on the forward gun mount. A leak developed in the conning tower eyepiece and was repaired.

Patrol 6 Commanding Officer Lt Cmdr B.F. McMahon

7 June 1943 Left Brisbane
8 June While on training exercises with escort, the port motor controller failed again.
9 June Blew gasket on negative tank flood valve
15 June Sighted Buka Island and later Feni Island no enemy activity.
16 June On station
17 June Attack #1 0200 Sighted 3 cargo ships at 20,000 yards, commenced tracking with radar, 0548 submerged and started closing track, 0625 sighted two freighters and a destroyer at 10,000 yards, manned battle stations. 0655 fired 4 torpedoes from aft tubes and went deep, 3 hits, 0702 first depth charges, 6 close astern overhead forcing boat down 15 feet to 310 feet. 0811 last two depth charges distant.
23 June Serviced torpedoes, found one exploder flooded, disabled magnetic exploder.
24 June 0009 Sighted two dark objects but nothing on radar, possibly a patrolling destroyer or the USS Greenling, could not identify and cleared area.
6 July Sighted floating mine, exploded with gun fire, a junior officer was struck with a piece of shrapnel receiving a scratch on a finger.
7 July 1330 Heard echo ranging from about 38,000 yards and then screw noise, starting closing. 1357 sighted aircraft over target area, 1411 sighted masts and stack of tanker at about 14,000 yards, 1515 secured from battle stations, could not close.
8 July Sighted a hospital ship
14 July 0920 Sighted smoke, 1022 sighted masts of four ships, manned battle stations, at a range of 6500 yards the contacts turned away, secured battle stations, could not get in position
19 July 0236 Sighted Green Island, 1145 sighted four engine patrol plane.
20 July 0522 Received orders to search for RAAF life raft. 0730 sighted enemy submarine on service at ten miles because of heavy black smoke, he dropped astern and disappeared. search for life raft, not found
21 July Leave station
26 July Arrive Brisbane

4 Torpedoes fired 3 hits

Experienced problems with #2 Aux generator, would not stop.
Problems with starboard distilling plant attributed to poor tender overhaul. A plug blew out on the trim pump and could not be replaced until an access hole was cut into the bulkhead between radio storage and the pump room, Port motor field interlock failed. Starboard shaft seal leaks excessive. Port reduction gear oil cooler leaked. Negative tank flood valve gasket blew out again,(negative tank is a variable ballast tank is used to aid surfacing and diving). Problems with all engines governors causing them to hunt.

Weather was mostly calm with glassy seas, not good for submarine operations.
There were several severe colds and three minor cases of "Vincents Agina", the quality of the food was not up to standards.

17 June sank passenger/cargo Myoko Maru 5,087 Tons

Duration of patrol 50 days, on station 36 days.
The Crew for the sixth patrol 1 new officer, 20 new enlisted men

Captain
McMahon, Bernard F.	LCdr Captain
Rindskopf, Maurice H.	Lt. Exec
Harper, John D.	Lt
Ramsing Verner U.	Ltjg.
Young, C. M.	Ltjg
Pridonoff, Eugene	Ltjg
Hazapis, T.	Ens.
Alamia, Anthony J.	MoMM2c
Allen, Frank L.	F2c
Anderson, Robert L.	EM1c
Applegate, Elvin C.	TM1c
Armstrong, Kenneth G.	CEM
Baker, Nesbert D.	SC3c
Bell, Edgar A.	MoMM1c
Boldt, Charles W.	F2c
Brownell, Ralph E.	MoMM2c
Burke, John A.	EM2c
Carr, Roy Jr.	TM3c
Carmean, Myrlon H.	TM3c
Corbett, Glenn C.	EM3c
Crowe, Audley L.	CGM
Dalwitz, Wailbert, W.	F1c
Decoo, George F.	YM1c
DeGrazio, Tony	CSM
Dozier, Henry M.	MoMM1c
Eksterowicz, Edward	F2c
Eller, Dock M.	CMoMM
Eubanks, James W.	F2c
Fedor, Robert C.	RM3c
Fox, Conrad L.	EM3c
Galas, Alexander	SM1c
Harris, Caleb S.	SC3c
Helgerson, Joseph	S1c
Heller, Jack E.	EM1c
Henderson, Lee	SC2c
Ireland, Joe N.	RM2c
Kane, Thomas P. Jr.	S1c
Kearns, Glenn E.	S2c
Kissinger, Robert	TM3c
Krooner, Edward W.	MoMM1c
Lang, Emerson	MoMM1c
Lamfers, Albert W.	S1c
Leach, Gilbert E.	MoMM1c

Lytle, George W.	OFck2c
Macarelli, Joseph S.	F2c
May, Maynard D.	PhM1c
McCowan, James L.	TM3c
Meyer, John J.	TM3c
Owens, Hardy B.	CMoMM
Pettigrew, Rex L.	MoMM2c
Phillips, Rollie P.	S1c
Pyle, Clarence L.	TM1c
Reed, Gordon M.	S2c
Rich, Jack M.	MoMM2c
Ritchie, Robert W.	F1c
Rowe, James E.	S2c
Ruebush, Calvin P.	S1c
Royal, Arthur M.	StM1c
Schaedler, George A.	EM1c
Simko, Frank M.	F1c
Smith, Alvah P.	EM3c
Smith Andrew J.	GM2c
Stover, Rual C.	S1c
Straight, John E.	F2c
Style, Norman V.	RM2c
Sullenger, James M.	FC1c
Swope, William R.	RM2c
Szymanski, Ted	GM3c
Vaughan, Donald O.	RM3c
Watson, James D.	SM2c
Webber, James F.	MoMM2c
Wentz, Royce E.	GM2c
White Raymond F.	TM2c
White, Robert E.	MoMM2c
Whitright, Earl B.	EM2c
Workman, Thomas M.	TM2c

Seven Officers and Sixty nine Enlisted

Eighteen men transferred off after sixth patrol

Harper, John D.	Lt Silver Star Navy Commendation Harper was lost with the Shark II
Alamia, Anthony J.	MoMM2c
Armstrong, Kenneth G.	CEM
Baker, Nesbert D.	SC3c
Bell, Edgar A.	MoMM1c
Brownwell, Ralph E.	MoMM2c

Carmean, Myrlon H.	TM3c	Navy Commendation
Dalwitz, Wailbert, W.	F1c	
Fedor, Robert C.	RM3c	
Galas, Alexander	SM1c	
Meyer, John J.	TM3c	
Pettigrew, Rex L.	MoMM2c	
Reed, Gordon M.	S2c	
Ritchie, Robert W.	F1c	
Rowe, James E.	S2c	
Royal, Arthur M.	StM1c	
Smith Andrew J.	GM2c	
Stover, Rual C.	S1c	
Style, Norman V.	RM2c	

SEVENTH PATROL

Seventh Patrol

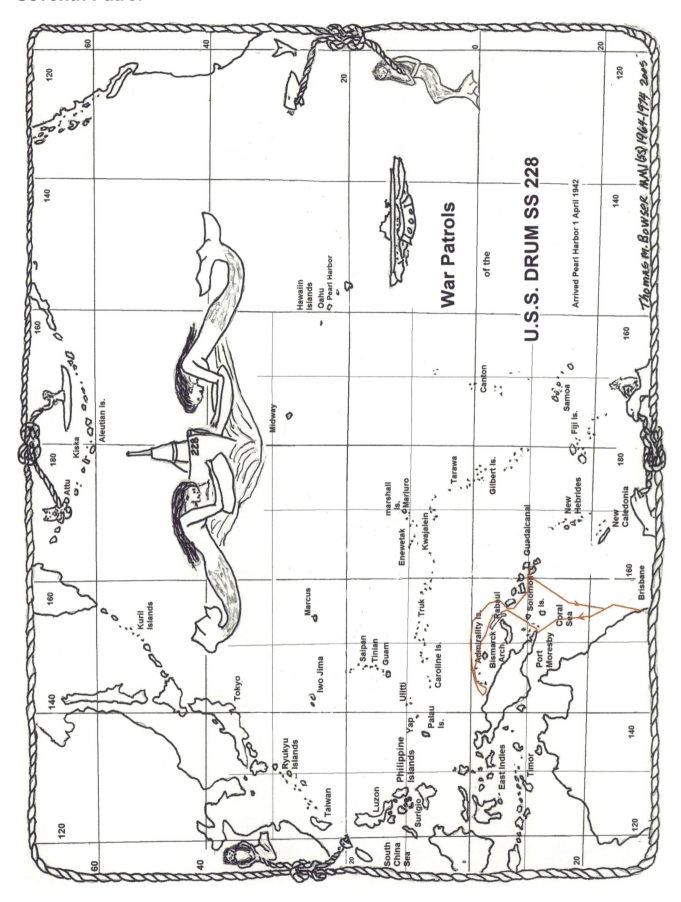

During normal 3 week refit an access hole and cover was installed between radio storage and the pump room, behind the trim pump, to aid in maintenance of the trim pump. Port motor field interlock replaced.

Patrol #7 Commanding Officer McMahon

11 August 1943 Left Brisbane with USS Bowfin and USS Tuna, for independent Patrol near Admiralty
    Islands
21 August Stopped in Jomard entrance New Guinea to refuel from USS Coucal
24-28 August Sighted many enemy aircraft.
26 August Found a leaking air flask in the torpedo tube #5, will replace tomorrow if not used.
27 August 1045 sighted smoke of three ships, two merchants and one escort. Believed to be
    heading away, did not attempt to close. 1545 sighted smoke of four merchants and two
    escorts, could not surface during daylight and pursue. 2019 surfaced and commenced closing
    convoy.
28 August 0030 Manned battle stations. Attack #1, 0054 after ship of convoy turned on a search
    light, fired 4 torpedoes forward, submerged with escort 2500 yards off, 0055 fired two more
    tubes forward at second target, heard three torpedoes hit, depth charged, three close knocking
    cork loose as they passed 230 feet. Depth charging lasted until 0226 0515 surfaced and
    cleared area.
29 August 0858 Sighted smoke at 20,000 yards, commenced approach. 0922 manned battle
    stations. Attack #2, 0959 fired 3 torpedoes, no hits
31 August Sighted two small merchants could not close.
8 September 1158 Sighted smoke at 16,000 yards and commenced approach. 1244 Manned
    battle stations, Attack #3, 1336 fired 3 torpedoes from aft tubes, 1 hit ship sunk. 1432 sighted
    small freighter towing sampans, commenced approach, at 800 yards ship turned towards and an
    aircraft dropped bombs at us, cleared area. 1800 Had an 8 layered birthday cake for
    Lytle G.W.C1c
23 September End of patrol
29 September Stopped at Tulagi, transferred fuel and food to USS Guardfish
30 September Gave gyro parts to USS Gato, wait for replacements.
2 October Left Tulagi
6 October Arrive Brisbane

12 Torpedoes fired, 7 hits

7696 miles, 2390 miles in area

8 September sank cargo Hakutestsu Maru #13 1,134 Tons
    Damaged two others

Problems: Target Bearing Transmitters did not work, Pitomer quit 17 September
Salt water in starboard reduction gear oil, problems with the evaporator,
Finally no problems with port motor field interlock

Food was much better and crew had coca-cola syrup which they mixed with water and iced up in chill box.

Duration of patrol 51, on station 24 days.

The Crew for the seventh patrol 1 new officer, 15 new enlisted men

  Captain
McMahon, Bernard F.	LCdr Captain
Rindskopf, Maurice H.	Lt. Exec
Ramsing Verner U.	Ltjg.
Young, C. M.	Ltjg
Pridonoff, Eugene	Ltjg
Hazapis, T.	Ltjg.
Hanks, William E.	Ens.
Allen, Frank L.	F2c
Anderson, Robert L.	EM1c
Applegate, Elvin C.	TM1c
Boldt, Charles W.	TM3c
Burke, John A.	EM2c
Carr, Roy Jr.	TM3c
Corbett, Glenn C.	EM3c
Crowe, Audley L.	CGM
Curtis, Warren G.	SM2c
Dawson Elijah Jr.	OfCK3c
Decoo, George F.	YM1c
DeGrazio, Tony	CSM
DeRosa, Gerard J.	S1c
Dozier, Henry M.	MoMM1c
Eksterowicz, Edward	F2c
Eller, Dock M.	CMoMM
Eubanks, James W.	F2c
Fellow, Everett N.	SC1c
Fox, Conrad L.	EM3c
Harris, Caleb S.	SC3c
Helgerson, Joseph	S1c
Heller, Jack E.	EM1c
Henderson, Lee	SC2c
Hudson, John E.	S2c
Ireland, Joe N.	RM1c
Johnson, Charles H.	S2c
Johnson, Russell L.	S2c
Jones, Arthur	S1c
Kane, Thomas P. Jr.	TM3c
Kash, Arthur	S1c
Kearns, Glenn E.	S2c
Kissinger, Robert	TM2c
Krooner, Edward W.	MoMM1c
Lang, Emerson	MoMM1c

Lamfers, Albert W.	S1c
Leach, Gilbert E.	MoMM1c
Lytle, George W.	OFck2c
Macarelli, Joseph S.	F2c
May, Maynard D.	PhM1c
McCowan, James L.	TM3c
McIntire, Kenneth E.	S1c
Owens, Hardy B.	CMoMM
Phillips, Rollie P.	S1c
Pisarczyk, Frank	F3c
Pyle, Clarence L.	CTM
Rich, Jack M.	MoMM1c
Ruebush, Calvin P.	S1c
Schaedler, George A.	CEM
Simko, Frank M.	MoMM2c
Smith, Alvah P.	EM3c
Straight, John E.	F2c
Sullenger, James M.	FC1c
Swope, William R.	RM2c
Szymanski, Ted	GM3c
Talbot Verne M.	F2c
Thibideau, Ronald W.	EM3c
Vaughan, Donald O.	RM1c
Wajda, Steve J.	MoMM2c
Watson, James D.	SM2c
Webber, James F.	MoMM2c
Wentz, Royce E.	GM2c
White Raymond F.	TM2c
White, Robert E.	MoMM2c
Whitright, Earl B.	EM1c
Williamson, Phillip L.	TM3c
Workman, Thomas M.	TM2c
Wright, Lowell S.	MoMM1c

Seven Officers and Sixty Seven Enlisted

Fourteen men transferred off after seventh patrol

McMahon, Bernard F.	LCdr Captain	Navy Cross -Navy Commendation- Silver Star
Corbett, Glenn C.	EM3c	
Curtis, Warren G.	SM2c	
Decoo, George F.	YM1c	
Dozier, Henry M.	MoMM1c	Navy/Marine Medal
Fellow, Everett N.	SC1c	
Harris, Caleb S.	SC3c	
Heller, Jack E.	EM1c	
Kearns, Glenn E.	S2c	
Krooner, Edward W.	MoMM1c	
McIntire, Kenneth E.	S1c	
Straight, John E.	F2c	
Vaughan, Donald O.	RM1c	Silver Star
White Raymond F.	TM2c	Silver Star

EIGHTH PATROL

Eighth Patrol

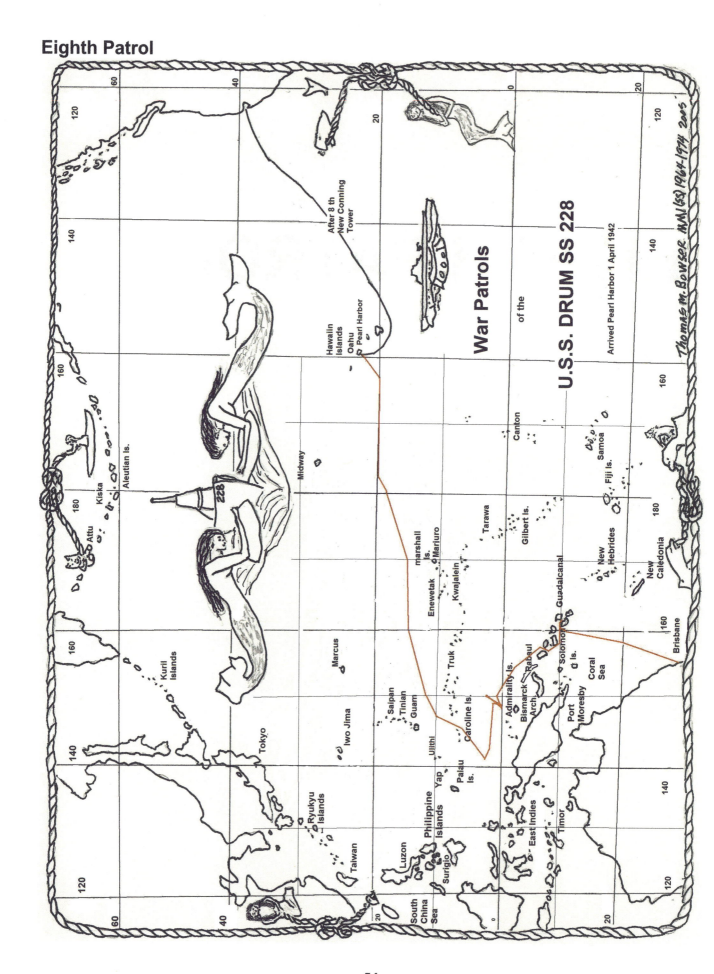

Normal 3 week refit. Dry docked for painting.

Patrol 8 Commanding Officer Cmdr D.F. Williamson

2 November 1943 Left Brisbane to patrol near the Bismarck Archipelago
7 November At Tulagi for fuel and water
9 November Arrived in area
11 November 0605 Sighted convoy at 18,000 yards, submerged and commenced approach, manned battle stations. 0625 identified convoy as three merchants and three escorts. 0710 fired 6 torpedoes, 1 torpedo premature at 500 yards, went deep, 2 hits. Depth charged, fuel oil leak aft engine room put 500 gals in bilge
12 November Sighted USS Albacore
13 November 1010 Sighted mast and stack of what looks like large tanker at 25,000 yards, commenced submerged approach but lost contact due to many rain squalls.
15 November 0150 Sighted three ships, possible war ships, tried to track but lost in rain squalls.
17 November 0310 Sighted a surfaced submarine, possibly USS Scamp both turned away and cleared.1140 spotted smoke from three ships at 24,000 yards, commenced tracking, 1327 manned battle stations. 1440 fired 4 torpedoes, went deep, 1 hit, depth charged, 1550 last depth charge no major damage. Returned to area of attack but could not get in position, cleared area.
18 November Sighted USS Blackfish, cruised with them for three hours while retuning radars.
19 November 0958 Sighted masts of three ships, closed to discover small trawler types towing barges and armed with deck guns, cleared area, did not rate torpedoes.
22 November 0907 Sighted smoke of three ships at 30,000 yards commenced tracking and determined to be four cargo ships. 1003 submerged and commenced approach, manned battle stations. 1137 fired 4 torpedoes, went deep, no hits, depth charged, conning tower aft door cracked, leaking 3-5 gallons/min, maneuvering room hard patch leaking
23 November Left station for Pearl Harbor
5 December Arrived Pearl Harbor. Pearl tried to repair conning tower but it started to buckle on test dive, it was decided to send boat to Mare Island.
9 January Left Pearl for Mare Island, arrived Mare Island 16 January
Left Mare Island 22 March, arrived Pearl Harbor 29 March

14 torpedoes fired, 3 hits

Sank cargo ship Hie Maru 11,930 Tons

9,617 miles in transit Brisbane to area and then to Pearl, 3672 miles on station
Duration of patrol 31 days, on station 14 days.

Still having problems with #2 Aux Generator

Pearl harbor, conning tower aft bulkhead removed, new one without door welded in place. During test dive to depth the conning tower buckled, the Drum was sent back to Mare Island shipyard in California.

The Crew for the Eighth patrol 3 new officers including CO, 15 new enlisted men

Williamson, D. F.	Cdr	Captain
Rindskopf, Maurice H.	LCdr	Exec
Young, C. M.	Lt	
Ramsing Verner U.	Lt.	
Pridonoff, Eugene	Ltjg	
Hazapis, T.	Ltjg.	
Hanks, William E.	Ens.	
Adams, O. B.	Ens	
Stemph, Charles R.	Ens	

Allen, Frank L.	F2c
Anderson, Robert L.	EM1c
Applegate, Elvin C.	TM1c
Bell, Edgar A.	MoMM1c
Boldt, Charles W.	F2c
Burke, John A.	EM1c
Brownell, Ralph E.	MoMM2c
Carmean, Myrlon H.	TM2c
Carr, Roy Jr.	TM2c
Crowe, Audley L.	CGM
Dawson Elijah Jr.	OfCK3c
DeGrazio, Tony	CSM
DeRosa, Gerard J.	S1c
Eksterowicz, Edward	F2c
Eller, Dock M.	CMoMM
Elkins, William C.	S1c
Eubanks, James W.	F1c
Fox, Conrad L.	EM3c
Helgerson, Joseph	S1c
Henderson, Lee	SC2c
Hudson, John E.	S2c
Johnson, Charles H.	S2c
Johnson, Russell L.	S2c
Jones, Arthur	RM3c
Kane, Thomas P. Jr.	TM3c
Kash, Arthur	GM3c
Kissinger, Robert	TM2c
Kronholm, Donald E.	S2c
Lang, Emerson	MoMM1c
Lamfers, Albert W.	S1c
Langkil, Lawrence L.	S2c
Leach, Gilbert E.	MoMM1c
Lytle, George W.	OFck1c
Macarelli, Joseph S.	F2c
May, Maynard D.	PhM1c
McCowan, James L.	TM3c
Meyer, John J.	TM3c
Owens, Hardy B.	CMoMM

Phillips, Rollie P.	S1c
Pisarczyk, Frank	F3c
Pyle, Clarence L.	CTM
Rich, Jack M.	MoMM1c
Robbins, Jack R.	EM2c
Ruebush, Calvin P.	S1c
Schaedler, George A.	CEM
Scheiking, Walter D.	F2c
Serrand, Angelo A.	F1c
Simko, Frank M.	MoMM2c
Smith, Alvah P.	EM3c
Sullenger, James M.	CFC
Swope, William R.	RM2c
Szymanski, Ted	GM3c
Talbot Verne M.	F2c
Thibideau, Ronald W.	EM3c
Tomaselli, Jake	EM3c
Wajda, Steve J.	MoMM2c
Watson, James D.	SM1c
Webber, James F.	MoMM1c
Wentz, Royce E.	GM2c
White, Robert E.	MoMM2c
Whitright, Earl B.	EM1c
Williamson, Phillip L.	TM3c
Wolf, William H.	SC3c
Wood, Lester M.	YM2c
Workman, Thomas M.	TM1c
Wright, James D.	EM3c
Wright, Lowell S.	MoMM1c
Zimmerman, Robert C.	SM2c

Nine Officers and Sixty Eight Enlisted

Twenty one men transferred off after eighth patrol

Bell, Edgar A.	MoMM1c	
Burke, John A.	EM1c	
Brownwell, Ralph E.	MoMM2c	
Dawson Elijah Jr.	OfCK3c	
Eller, Dock M.	CMoMM	Silver Star
Henderson, Lee	SC2c	Navy Commendation
Ireland, Joe N.	RM2c	
Kane, Thomas P. Jr.	TM3c	
Macarelli, Joseph S.	F2c	

May, Maynard D.	PhM1c
McCowan, James L.	TM3c
Owens, Hardy B.	CMoMM
Pyle, Clarence L.	TM1c
Schaedler, George A.	CEM
Scheiking, Walter D.	F2c
Serrand, Angelo A.	F1c
Sullenger, James M.	FC1c Silver Star
Webber, James F.	MoMM1c
Wolf, William H.	SC3c
Wood, Lester M.	YM2c
Wright, Lowell S.	MoMM1c

NINTH PATROL

Ninth Patrol

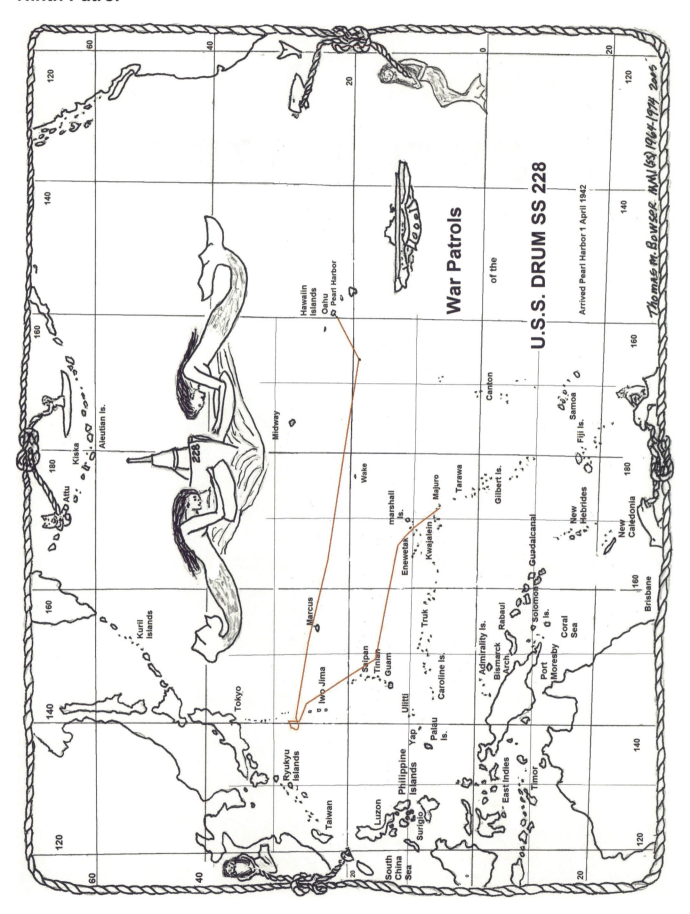

At Mare Island the conning tower was replaced with one from the new class of submarines, the Balao class and the new tower was rated for 400' test depth while the rest of the boat was still rated for 300'. The fairwater was again modified with the new "trigger" style bridge, the high pressure air compressors were replaced with "gar" compressors, the bathythermograph was moved into control, and the state rooms were rearranged; the captain's stateroom got an 8 ½" 165' depth gage. JP sound gear installed

Patrol 9 Commanding Officer Cdr Williamson

9 April 1944 Left Pearl Harbor to area near Iwo Jima
10 April 2200 Leach G. E. MoMM1c discovered a crack in a circular weld in the overhead in the after engine room, the crack was in the weld of a plate that was put in at Mare Island after degaussing the boat, the crack was all the way around the plate but did not leak when submerged.
11 April At Johnston Island, took on fuel and food, repaired crack in hull plate in aft engine room. Tied up alongside the USS Sturgeon and USS Tambor pulled alongside the Drum.
12 April 0620 Under way with Tambor
18 April 1030 Sighted smoke with Tambor alongside a burning spitkit. Tambor took two prisoners.
20 April North of Marcus Island
22 April Near Iwo Jima
19 May Depth charged by air craft while surfacing, no damage
31 May Arrived Majuro Island

No torpedoes fired

12,641 total miles 6,233 miles in area

The weather and water temperatures were mild and so it was fairly comfortable inside.

Duration of patrol 52 days, on station 31days.

The Drum did not run into any targets of opportunity on this patrol but spotted many aircraft from both sides, lots of trawlers and patrol boats.

The Crew for the Ninth patrol 3 new officers, 22 new enlisted men

Williamson, D. F.	Cdr	Captain
Rindskopf, Maurice H.	LCdr	Exec
Young, C. M.	Lt	
Ramsing Verner U.	Lt.	
Pridonoff, Eugene	Lt	
Hazapis, T.	Ltjg.	

Hanks, William E.	Ltjg.
Adams, O. B.	Ens
Stemph, Charles R.	Ens
Roach, D. F.	Ens
Sullenger, James M.	Ens
Schaedler, George A.	Ens
Allen, Frank L.	MoMM2c
Anderson, Robert L.	EM1c
Applegate, Elvin C.	CTM2
Baker, James E.	F1c
Boldt, Charles W.	MoMM3c
Brown, James C.	S1c
Carmean, Myrlon H.	TM2c
Carr, Roy Jr.	TM2c
Chico, Dominick P.	S1c
Crowe, Audley L.	CGM
DeGrazio, Tony	CSM
DeRosa, Gerard J.	Bkr3c
Dixon, Donald T.	S1c
Eksterowicz, Edward	MoMM2c
Elkins, William C.	GM3c
Eubanks, James W.	MoMM1c
Fox, Conrad L.	EM2c
Foxworthy, Leland D.	S1c
Frederick, Clayton Jr.	S1c
Fry, Clyde C.	SC2c
Furman, Phillip A.	MM1c
Green, Wayne S. II	RT2c
Helgerson, Joseph	SM4c
Hudson, John E.	S1c
Johnson, Charles H.	YM1c
Johnson, Russell L.	S1c
Jones, Arthur	RM2c
Kalamen, Paul	EM1c
Kash, Arthur	GM3c
Kellett, George W.	SC1c
Killough, Walter J.	CMoMM
Kissinger, Robert	TM2c
Kronholm, Donald E.	S1c
Lang, Emerson	MoMM1c
Lamfers, Albert W.	S1c
Langkil, Lawrence L.	F1c
La Beuf, Alfred W.	RT3c
Lazo, Edward	S1c
Leach, Gilbert E.	MoMM1c
Lister, William E.	RM3c
Lytle, George W.	OFck1c
McFadden, Ralph W.	PhM1c
McKay, Claude J.	StM2c

Meyer, John J.	TM2c
Mossing, William F.	MoMM2c
Phillips, Rollie P.	TM3c
Pisarczyk, Frank	MoMM3c
Rich, Jack M.	MoMM1c
Robbins, Jack R.	EM2c
Ruebush, Calvin P.	TM3c
Rodgers, Charles	S2c
Simko, Frank M.	MoMM1c
Smith, Alvah P.	EM2c
Steele, Creinghton S.	MoMM1c
Stout, Claude G.	CEM
Swope, William R.	RM2c
Szymanski, Ted	GM2c
Talbot Verne M.	MoMM1c
Thibideau, Ronald W.	EM3c
Tomaselli, Jake	EM3c
Wajda, Steve J.	MoMM1c
Walsh, Thomas E.	EM3c
Watson, James D.	SM1c
Wentz, Royce E.	GM2c
White, Robert E.	MoMM1c
Whitright, Earl B.	EM1c
Williamson, Phillip L.	TM2c
Workman, Thomas M.	TM1c
Wright, James D.	EM3c
Zimmerman, Robert C.	SM2c

Twelve Officers and Seventy Enlisted

Fourteen men transferred off after Ninth patrol

Williamson, D. F.	Cdr	Captain	Silver Star
Ramsing Verner U.	Lt	Bronze Star-Navy Commendation	
Schaedler, George A.	Ens		

Allen, Frank L.	MoMM3c
Anderson, Robert L.	EM1c Navy/ Marine Medal
Boldt, Charles W.	MoMM3c
Carr, Roy Jr.	TM2c
Crowe, Audley L.	CGM Silver Star
Hudson, John E.	S1c
Lang, Emerson	MoMM1c
Leach, Gilbert E.	MoMM1c Bronze Star
Rodgers, Charles	S2c
Szymanski, Ted	GM2c Received Navy/Marine Commendation Medal
Talbot Verne M.	F2c
Thibideau, Ronald W.	EM3c
Whitright, Earl B.	EM1c Navy/ Marine Medal

TENTH PATROL

Tenth Patrol

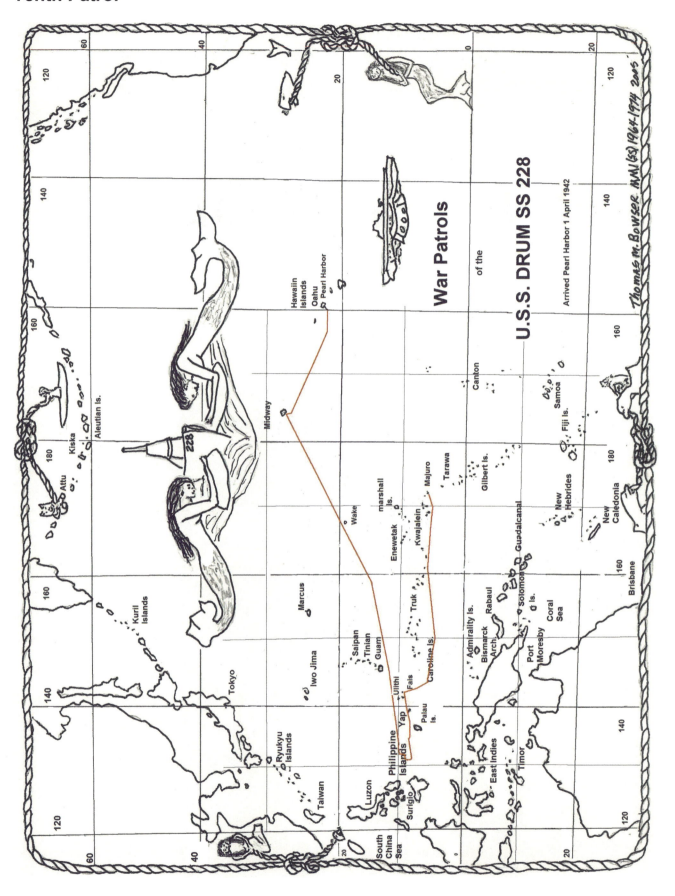

Normal 3 week refit

Patrol 10 Commanding Officer LCdr M.H. Rindskopf. Cdr Williamson was taken ill before the tenth patrol and LCdr Rindskopf was asked if wanted to work under another skipper or take over the job himself. He of course took the job. (Rindskopf was part of the original commissioning crew and was the youngest submarine captain at 26. He would complete 11 war patrols on the Drum).

While at Majuro Drum made its first acquaintance with the battleship USS Alabama BB-60 which was in the harbor at the same time, Drum would later be reunited with the Alabama at Battleship Memorial Park in Mobile, Al in 1969 where she would become the first submarine to be opened as a museum.

24 June 1944 Left Majuro for the Palau Islands east of the Philippines
1 July Off Yap Island on station
3 July Watched U.S. bombers attack Yap and being attacked by fighters afterwards, one of the fighters spotted the Drum and strafed, minor damage to deck, and all radio antenna wires hit but not broken.
4 July 2205 Opened fire on Refinery point, Fais Island with 4" Gun to celebrate the 4th. Submariners find unusual ways to entertain themselves.
22 July Sighted convoy, fired 4 torpedoes, no hits
29 July Sank sampan with USS Blackfish, picked up 2 prisoners. Found salt water in port reduction gear. Ordered back to Pearl
10 August At Midway for fuel
14 August Arrive Pearl Harbor

4 torpedoes fired no hits

12,894 total miles 6,182 miles on station

Duration of patrol 51days, on station 31days.

The whole time on station there was daily sightings of enemy aircraft and no shipping other than small stuff. The prisoners were separated to each torpedo room and kept under guard, one eventually became a mess cook washing dishes and the other wiped down the engine rooms, the sampan they came off of had 100 soldiers on board.

The Crew for the Tenth patrol 2 new officers, 12 new enlisted men

Rindskopf, Maurice H.	LCdr	Captain
Young, C. M.	Lt	
.Johnson, W. H.	Ltjg	
Pridonoff, Eugene	Lt	
Nelson, R. E.	Ltjg	
Hazapis, T.	Ltjg.	
Hanks, William E.	Ltjg.	
Adams, O. B.	Ltjg	
Stemph, Charles R.	Ltjg	
Roach, D. F.	Ens	
Sullenger, James M.	Ens	

Applegate, Elvin C.	CTM
Baker, James E.	F1c
Bledsoe, James F.	S1c
Brown, James C.	S1c
Carmean, Myrlon H.	TM1c
Chico, Dominick P.	S1c
Cozier, Charles S.	EM3c
Crowe, Ray A.	MoMM2c
DeGrazio, Tony	CSM
DeRosa, Gerard J.	Bkr3c
Dixon, Donald T.	S1c
Doran, Hugh J. III	FSC3c
Eksterowicz, Edward	MoMM2c
Elkins, William C.	GM3c
Eubanks, James W.	MoMM2c
Fooks, Raymond	F1c
Fox, Conrad L.	EM1c
Foxworthy, Leland D.	S1c
Frederick, Clayton Jr.	S1c
Fry, Clyde C.	SC2c
Furman, Phillip A.	CMoMM
Green, Wayne S. II	RT2c
Helgerson, Joseph	SM3c
Hutchinson, Morris	EM3c
Jacobson, Gerald C.	S1c
Johnson, Charles H.	YM1c
Johnson, Russell L.	TM3c
Jones, Arthur	RM2c
Kalamen, Paul	CEM
Kash, Arthur	QM3c
Kellett, George W.	SC1c
Killough, Walter J.	CMoMM
Kissinger, Robert	TM2c
Kronholm, Donald E.	S1c
Lamfers, Albert W.	TM3c
Langkil, Lawrence L.	MoMM3c
La Beuf, Alfred W.	RT3c
Lazo, Edward	S1c
Lister, William E.	RM3c
Lytle, George W.	OFck1c
McFadden, Ralph W.	PhM1c
McKay, Claude J.	StM2c
Meyer, John J.	TM2c
Mossing, William F.	MoMM2c
Mullen, John T.	EM3c
Nielson, Russell H.	MoMM3c
Olson, Carroll A.	F2c
Phillips, Rollie P.	TM3c
Pisarczyk, Frank	MoMM2c

Rich, Jack M.	MoMM1c
Robbins, Jack R.	EM1c
Ruebush, Calvin P.	TM3c
Simko, Frank M.	MoMM1c
Smith, Alvah P.	EM1c
Steele, Creinghton S.	MoMM1c
Stout, Claude G.	CEM
Swope, William R.	RM2c
Tomaselli, Jake	EM2c
Valenzuela, E. T.	MoMM1c
Wajda, Steve J.	MoMM1c
Walsh, Thomas E.	EM2c
Watson, James D.	SM1c
Watt, James B.	EM3c
Wentz, Royce E.	S1c
Wheeler, Hubert	EM3c
White, Robert E.	MoMM1c
Williamson, Phillip L.	TM2c
Workman, Thomas M.	TM1c
Wright, James D.	EM2c
Zimmerman, Robert C.	SM2c

Eleven Officers and Seventy Enlisted

Twelve men transferred off after Tenth patrol

Sullenger, James M.	Ens	Silver Star
Applegate, Elvin C.	CTM	Navy/Marine Medal
Dixon, Donald T.	S1c	
Eksterowicz, Edward	MoMM2c	
Helgerson, Joseph	Sm3c	
Jones, Arthur	RM2c	
Lazo, Edward	S1c	
Meyer, John J.	TM2c	
Robbins, Jack R.	EM1c	
Stout, Claude G.	CEM	
Swope, William R.	RM2c	

ELEVENTH PATROL

Eleventh Patrol

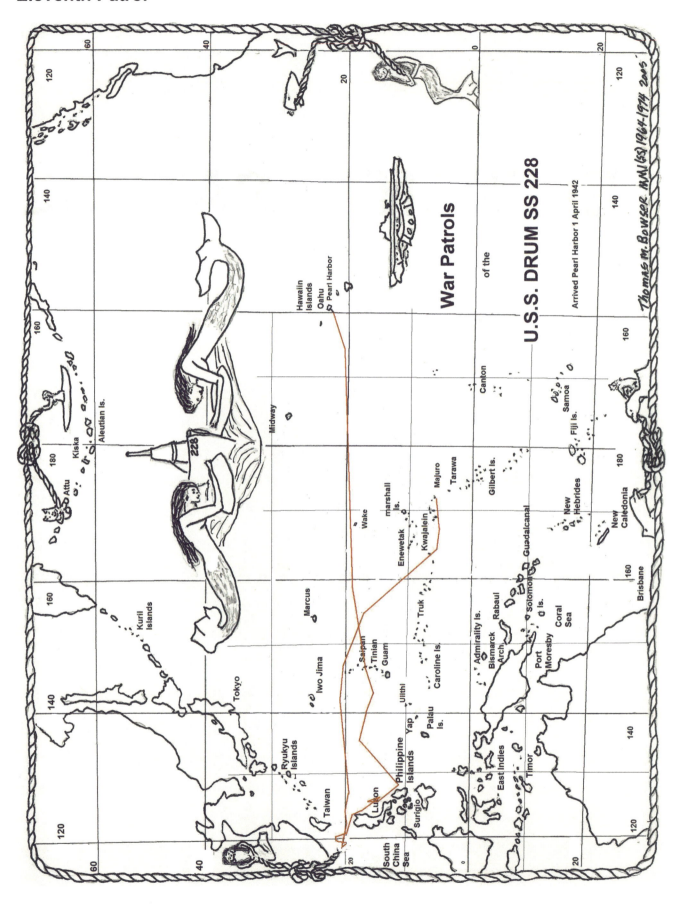

Normal 2 week refit. Fired MK 18 and MK 23 torpedoes for training. Air conditioning unit and booster fan installed in Control room. The Mark 18 torpedo was the first attempt at an electric torpedo and was a copy of a captured German torpedo; because they were electric they were wakeless. The Mark 23 torpedo was a single speed MK 14; it was used to speed up production of torpedoes.

Patrol 11 Commanding Officer Rindskopf

9 September 1944 1330 Left Pearl Harbor for area near Philippines, Surigao Straight, with USS Sawfish, USS Icefish, USS Rock and an escort. 1915 Rock and escort left company. Enroute to Saipan.
11 September #2 Aux broke Lower crank shaft 3 cylinder 150 KW
21 September Exchanged calls with west bound Pamanito 0335 radar contact with Parche. 1210 moored with Parche alongside tender Fulton, took on fuel, water and supplies and made minor repairs.
22 September Left Saipan with Sawfish, ordered to Surigio Strait
24 September Experiencing cavation port screw
26 September Blew negative tank flood valve gasket
28 September 0000 Made rendezvous with USS Gar and exchanged information.
12 October Crack in water jacket liner #2 main engine #1 cylinder does not affect operation of engine
14 October Plans were made for special celebration of 1,000 dive but Drum was attacked by aircraft while captain was asleep and the boat had to dive, also marking 140,000 miles at the same time
16 October On station but drifted north into Parche's area
17 October Exchanged signals with USS Seadragon
18 October Received orders to join up with Sawfish and Icefish.
23 October 1824 Surfaced to patrol to southwest as Sawfish and Icefish are to the west, 1905 made radar contact, determined to be 4 ships and 3 escorts, sent contact report. 2240 Icefish and Sawfish have contact and Snook is closing. 2330 Sawfish completed attack, heard six explosions.
24 October 0042 A roving escort closes to within 2700 yards does not spot Drum, 0107 sighted gunfire and explosions, Snook is making attack. Commenced approach on port side, Attack #1, fired 4 MK 18 torpedoes from aft 3200 yards, no hits, Trailing from port flank while Snook takes a turn, 0318 Snook reports done, two ships hit. 0330 start second attack, 0400 unable to close due to escorts, 0415-0615 trying to lose 4 escorts. 0619 finally shook escorts, dove. 0700 sighted freighter at 9,000 yards, commenced approach, Attack #2, 0705 sighted escort and three more cargos, 0750 heard 11 distand depth charges, 0757 fired 4 torpedoes forward, dove to evade, 3 hits, 13 depth charges not close. 0800-1215 sighted aircraft and escort, heard many distant depth charges, 1853 surfaced.
26 October 0020 Radar contact, reported to Icefish and Snook, determined to be 13 ships including 3 escorts. 0300 commenced Attack #3 0350 with an escort at 1100 yards, fired 6 torpedoes forward at two ships, 1 hit, turned to line up stern tubes, 0357 fired 4 MK 18 torpedoes aft at third ship at 3050 yard, 4 hits, 0430 completed reload recommenced attack, quickly maneuvered to get into position for a dawn submerged attack. 0555 submerged distance to track 5,000 yards, 0651 targets zigged towards Drum, 0652 fired 4 torpedoes forward range 2100 yards, fired two more from forward, 4 hits. 0700-0925 prolonged depth charging, 51 counted no major damage

27 October Joined Sawfish and Seadragon to search for reported downed pilot in vicinity of Balintang Channel.
28 October After finding debris and empty raft joined up with Sawfish and traded 20 gals hydraulic oil for 100# of sugar.
29 October 0700 Still searching, 2100 depart area with Sawfish.
8 November Arrived Majuro.

8 MK 18 electric torpedoes fired from aft with 2 hits, this is the first use of the new MK 18 by the Drum

14 MK 23 torpedoes fired from fwd, 9 hits, this is the first use of the new MK 23 single speed steam torpedo by the Drum

2 MK 14 torpedoes fired from fwd, 1 hit
All torpedoes expended

24 Oct sank cargo/passenger ship Shikisan Maru 4,725 Tons
26 Oct sank cargo ship Taisho Maru 6,886 Tons
        cargo ship Taihaku Maru 6,886 Tons

14,325 total miles, 4,368 on station

Duration of patrol 59 days, on station 29 days.

Water temperature was 82-84 degrees down to 325 feet, hot inside boat.
It is rumored that the cook DeRosa (Skinny Ghinny) got too energetic chopping onions and forced the boat to surface to ventilate. It is also rumored that his first attempt at baking bread became quite interesting: the first batch wouldn't rise so he put it in a gunny sack and in the trash locker in the crew's mess, the second attempt meet the same fate, someone told him it takes time and about then the locker door exploded open with dough going everywhere; despite all this he is reported to be a good cook.

Crew for the Eleventh Patrol 3 new officers and eleven enlisted men

Rindskopf, Maurice H.	LCdr Captain
Young, C. M.	Lt
.Johnson, W. H.	Ltjg
Pridonoff, Eugene	Lt
Nelson, R. E.	Ltjg
Hazapis, T.	Ltjg.
Hanks, William E.	Ltjg.
Adams, O. B.	Ltjg
Stemph, Charles R.	Ens
Roach, D. F.	Ens
Connolly, P. J.	Ens
Bader, G. H.	Ens
Shonerd, W.	Ens
Abell, William K	S1c
Baker, James E.	MoMM3c

Birdsell, Donald A.	RM3c
Bledsoe, James F.	S1c
Boap, Emmett J.	TM1c
Brown, James C.	S1c
Carmean, Myrlon H.	TM1c
Champion, James R.	S1c
Chico, Dominick P.	FCS3c
Cozier, Charles S.	RM3c
Crowe, Ray L.	MoMM2c
DeGrazio, Tony	CSM
DeRosa, Gerard J.	Bkr3c
Dittmeyer, Jack L.	RM1c
Doran, Hugh J. III	FSC2c
Elkins, William C.	GM3c
Eubanks, James W.	MoMM2c
Fooks, Raymond	F1c
Fox, Conrad L.	EM1c
Foxworthy, Leland D.	TM3c
Frederick, Clayton Jr.	EM3c
Fry, Clyde C.	SC2c
Furman, Phillip A.	CMoMM
Green, Wayne S. II	RT2c
Hutchinson, Morris	EM2c
Jacobson, Gerald C.	S1c
Johnson, Charles H.	YM1
Johnson, Russell L.	TM3c
Kalamen, Paul	CEM
Kash, Arthur	GM2c
Kellett, George W.	SC1c
Killough, Walter J.	CMoMM
Kissinger, Robert	TM2c
Klosterman, Clarence J.	S2c
Kronholm, Donald E.	S1c
Lamfers, Albert W.	TM3c
Langkil, Lawrence L.	MoMM3c
La Beuf, Alfred W.	RT3c
Lefler, Kenneth C.	SM2c
Lister, William E.	RM3c
Lytle, George W.	OFck1c
Lund, Paul E.	F1c
Maledy, Kenneth L.	F1c
McFadden, Ralph W.	PhM1c
McKay, Claude J.	StM1c
Mossing, William F.	MoMM2c
Mullen, John T.	EM3c
Nielson, Russell H.	MoMM3c
Olson, Carroll A.	F1c
Phillips, Rollie P.	TM3c
Pisarczyk, Frank	MoMM2c
Powell, Frederick E.	F2c

Rich, Jack M.	MoMM1c
Ruebush, Calvin P.	TM3c
Simko, Frank M.	MoMM1c
Smith, Alvah P.	EM1c
Steele, Creinghton S.	MoMM1c
Tacke, Milton C.	RM3c
Talbot Verne M.	MoMM1c
Tomaselli, Jake	EM2c
Valenzuela, E. T.	MoMM1c
Wajda, Steve J.	MoMM1c
Walsh, Thomas E.	EM2c
Watson, James D.	SM1c
Watt, James B.	EM3c
Wentz, Royce E.	GM1
Wheeler, Hubert	EM3c
White, Robert E.	MoMM1c
Williamson, Phillip L.	TM2c
Workman, Thomas M.	TM1c
Wright, James D.	EM2c
Zimmerman, Robert C.	SM2c

Thirteen Officers and Seventy Two Enlisted

Fourteen men transferred off after Eleventh patrol. With the departure of LCdr Rindskopf the Drum would not hit another target.

Rindskopf, Maurice H.	LCdr	Captain	Navy Cross-Silver Star-Bronze Star-Navy Commendation- Legion of Merit
Hazapis, T.	Ltjg.	Bronze Star	
Hanks, William E.	Ltjg		
Shonerd, W.	Ens		
Abell, William K	S1c		
DeGrazio, Tony	CSM	Silver Star	
DeRosa, Gerard J.	Bkr3c		
Fooks, Raymond	F1c		
Lamfers, Albert W.	TM3c		
Lytle, George W.	OFck1c	Bronze Star	
Mullen, John T.	EM3c		
Rich, Jack M.	MoMM1c	Bronze Star	

Valenzuela, E. T.   MoMM1c
Wajda, Steve J.   MoMM1c
Workman, Thomas M.   TM1c   Navy/Marine Medal

TWELFTH PATROL

Twelfth Patrol

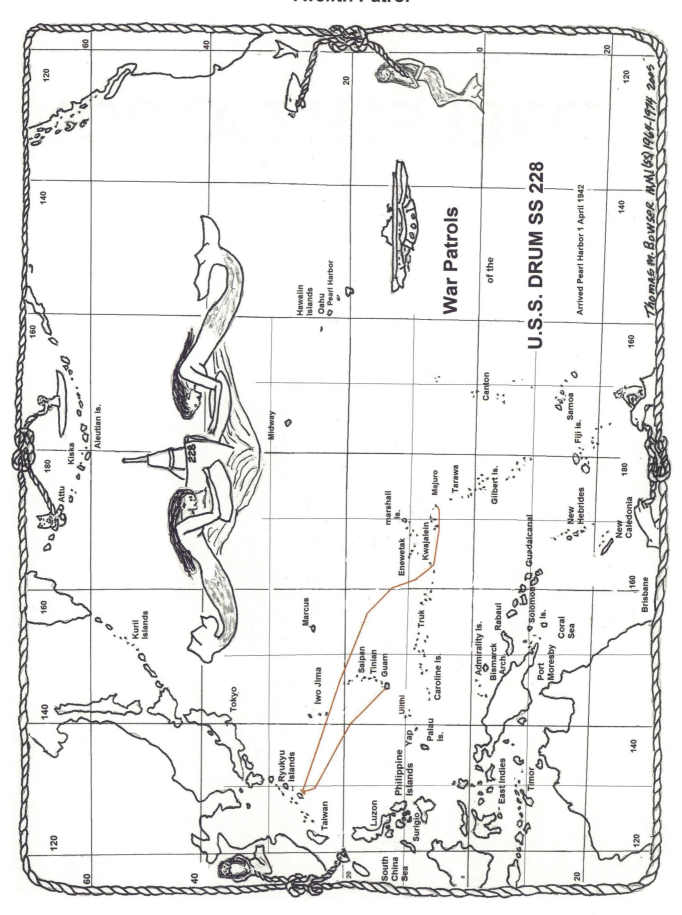

Normal 3 week refit. Dry docked twice for cavitation of port screw, screw was replaced. 2 MK 18 and 4 MK 23 torpedoes fired for training

Patrol 12 Commanding Officer Lt Cmdr Eddy
7 December 1944 Left Majuro for the Ryukyu Islands south of Japan
30 December 0635 Dove west of Gaja Shima, 1058 heard pinging, 1100 sighted smoke, 1115 manned battle stations commenced tracking, sighted masts of 5 freighters and 3 escorts, 1142 convoy at 7000 yards zigged left, 1203 range 2000 yards fired 6 Mk 18 forward, no hits, depth charged
13 January Departed station
17 January Arrived Guam

6 torpedoes fired, no hits 16 Mk 18 torpedoes were carried forward
Targets are getting sparse, lots of aircraft and patrol craft

3,462 miles to station
3,711 miles on station
1,298 miles to Guam

Duration of patrol 41days, on station 25 days.

Problems: Cracked water jacket liner #1 main engine #3 cylinder

Temperature inside boat was cool due to time of year and being further north than usual.

Crew for the Twelfth Patrol 1 new officer the Captain and Thirteen new enlisted men

Eddy, F. M.	LCdr	Captain
Young, C. M.	Lt	
Etheridge, W. R.	Lt	
Johnson, W. H.	Lt	
Pridonoff, Eugene	Lt	
Nelson, R. E.	Ltjg	
Adams, O. B.	Ltjg	
Stemph, Charles R.	Ltjg	
Roach, D. F.	Ltjg	
Connolly, P. J.	Ens	
Bader, G. H.	Ens	

Baker, James E.	MoMM3c
Barnett, George M.	F1c
Birdsell, Donald A.	RM3c
Bledsoe, James F.	S1c
Bloom, William	StM2c
Boap, Emmett J.	TM1c
Brown, James C.	S1c
Campbell, Robert M.	TM2c
Carmean, Myrlon H.	TM1c
Champion, James R.	S1c

Chico, Dominick P.	FCS3c
Cozier, Charles S.	RM3c
Cole, Percy	RM2c
Crowe, Ray A.	MoMM2c
Dittmeyer, Jack L.	RM1c
Dodd, Oliver L.	SC2c
Doran, Hugh J. III	FSC2c
Elkins, William C.	GM3c
Eubanks, James W.	MoMM3c
Fox, Conrad L.	EM1c
Foxworthy, Leland D.	TM3c
Fry, Clyde C.	SC2c
Furman, Phillip A.	CMoMM
Green, Wayne S. II	RT1c
Hutchinson, Morris	EM2c
Jacobson, Gerald C.	S1c
Johnson, Charles H.	YM1c
Johnson, Russell L.	TM3c
Kalamen, Paul	CEM
Kash, Arthur	GM2c
Killough, Walter J.	CMoMM
Kissinger, Robert	TM2c
Klosterman, Clarence J.	S2c
Kronholm, Donald E.	S1c
Kurtz, Leslie R.	SC3c
Langkil, Lawrence L.	MoMM3c
La Beuf, Alfred W.	RT3c
Lefler, Kenneth C.	SM2c
Levine, David H.	SM1c
Lister, William E.	RM2c
Lund, Paul E.	F1c
Maledy, Kenneth L.	F1c
McFadden, Ralph W.	PhM1c
McKay, Claude J.	StM1c
Mossing, William F.	MoMM2c
Nielson, Russell H.	MoMM3c
Olson, Carroll A.	F1c
Phillips, Rollie P.	TM2c
Pisarczyk, Frank	MoMM2c
Powell, Frederick E.	F1c
Ring, Herbert Jr.	S1c
Ruebush, Calvin P.	TM3c
Schechter, Charles	MoMM3c
Schmidt, David	S1c
Shackelford, Theodore E.	CTM
Simko, Frank M.	MoMM1c
Steele, Creinghton S.	MoMM1c
Sturr, Thomas Jr.	MoMM1c
Tacke, Milton C.	RM3c
Talbot Verne M.	MoMM2c

Telthorst, Vernon L.	EM3c
Tomaselli, Jake	EM2c
Walsh, Thomas E.	EM2c
Watson, James D.	SM1c
Watt, James B.	EM3c
Wentz, Royce E.	GM1c
Wheeler, Hubert	EM3c
White, Robert E.	MoMM1c
Williamson, Phillip L.	TM2c
Wright, James D.	EM2c
Yanik, William P.	F1c
Zimmerman, Robert C.	SM2c

Eleven Officers and Seventy Two Enlisted

Eighteen men transferred off after Twelfth patrol

Young, C. M.	Lt	Silver Star
Pridonoff, Eugene	Lt	Bronze Star
Stemph, Charles R.	Ltjg	

Carmean, Myrlon H.	TM1c	
Elkins, William C.	GM3c	
Fox, Conrad L.	EM1c	Navy Commendation
Frederick, Clayton Jr.	S1c	
Kash, Arthur	GM2c	
Kellett, George W.	SC1c	
Kronholm, Donald E.	S1c	
Phillips, Rollie P.	TM2c	
Ruebush, Calvin P.	TM3c	
Simko, Frank M.	MoMM1c	
Smith, Alvah P.	EM3c	Bronze Star
Watson, James D.	SM1c	Navy/Marine Medal
Wentz, Royce E.	GM1c	Navy/Marine Medal
White, Robert E.	MoMM1c	
Workman, Thomas M.	TM1c	

LCdr Maurice (Mike) Rindskopf was the youngest submarine Captain in the war, he was only 26. When he came on board he was eventually made weapons officer and for almost all of the patrols he operated the torpedo data computer (TDC) in the conning tower. It was used to compute the targets speed, range bearing and angle and it would tell the torpedo which angle to take when it left the tubes. The information that was observed from the periscope was fed into the TDC and adjustments made until it agreed with what the crew was seeing. The TDC's were top secret well into the sixties. Rindskopf would retire as a rear admiral and continue to give lectures at the Naval Academy in Annapolis up until just before he passed away in 2011. He visited the Drum in 2007 and when he came up the ladder he saluted the flag, turned to Lesley and I and said "when the hell are you going to fix the outside of this boat?", I had no doubt who he was, he was 88 at the time and went thru the boat like he was twenty.

THIRTEENTH PATROL

Thirteenth Patrol

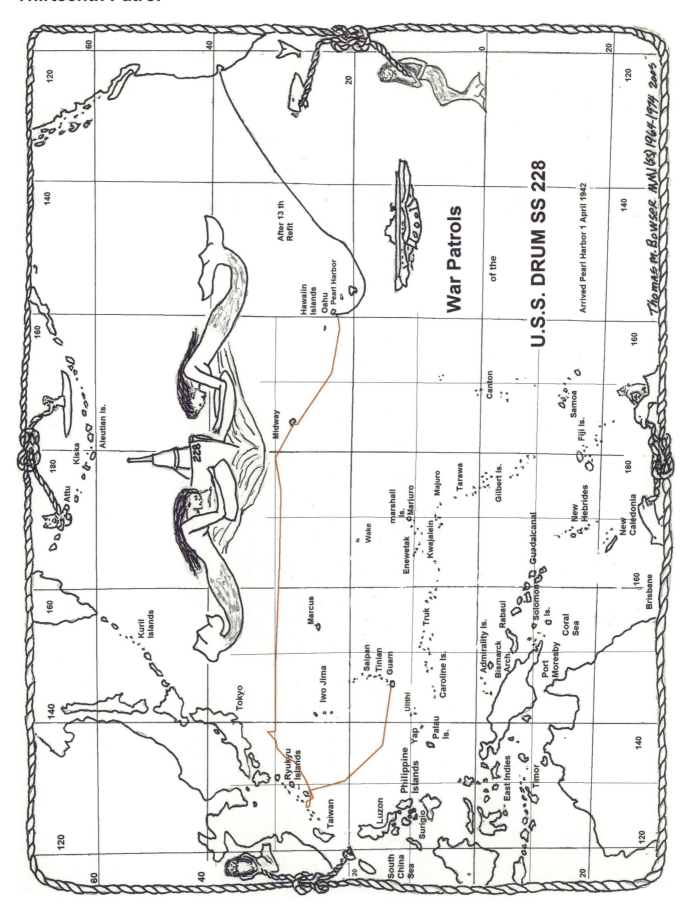

Normal 3 week refit

Patrol 13 Commanding Officer Eddy

11 February 1945 Left Guam for Ryukyu Islands
18 February Starboard reduction gear oil cooler leaks, repaired
7 March Sank floating mine
14 March Starboard reduction gear oil cooler leaks, repaired
22 March Left station
29 March Arrive Midway
2 April Arrive Pearl Harbor

No torpedoes fired, Most of the patrol was life guard duty for aircraft, their services were not required.

The crew experienced low grade food poisoning blamed on orange juice from California

The Drum had problems with both reduction gear oil coolers leaking sea water into the oil and spent a good bit of time repairing and changing out the coolers. Upon arrival in Pearl she also reported the superstructure was loose and making a racket. Also had problems with QB sonar..

The Drum was sent to Hunters Point shipyard in Calif. for major repairs and modification, she was there from 11 April- 11July 1945.
While at the shipyard she received the following modifications:
The cable hoists on the periscopes were replaced with hydraulic hoists
SJ radar moved aft, SD radar replaced with SV
4" gun removed 5" gun installed and a 40 mm replaced the forward 20
Install ammo scuttle aft of fairwater for 5" ammo
Replaced the trim manifold
Replaced the Gar air compressors with Hardi-Tynes
Installed washing machine
Modified bridge and fairwater
Installed Loran navigation
Installed Marker buoys which were later removed at Pearl Harbor

The Crew for the Thirteenth Patrol 2 new and Officers and 11 new enlisted men

Eddy, F. M.	LCdr	Captain
Etheridge, W. R.	Lt	
Johnson, W. H.	Lt	
Nelson, R. E.	Lt	
Adams, O. B.	Ltjg	
Roach, D. F.	Ltjg	
Connolly, P. J.	Ens	
Bader, G. H.	Ens	
Ryan, L. L.	Ens	
Korte, E. J.		
Baker, James E.	MoMM3c	

Barnett, George M.	F1c
Birdsell, Donald A.	RM3c
Bledsoe, James F.	S1c
Bloom, William	StM2c
Boap, Emmett J.	TM1c
Brown, James C.	S1c
Campbell, Robert M.	TM2c
Champion, James R.	S1c
Chico, Dominick P.	FCS3c
Cozier, Charles S.	EM2c
Cole, Percy	RM2c
Crowe, Ray A.	MoMM1c
Custer, Joseph W. Jr.	S1c
Dittmeyer, Jack L.	RM1c
Dodd, Oliver L.	SC2c
Doran, Hugh J. III	FSC2c
Dunphy, Joseph L.	MoMM1c
Echols, Albert	GM3c
Eubanks, James W.	MoMM2c
Fischer, Arthur C.	TM2c and his dog named Stateside
Fleischman, Russell	S1c
Foxworthy, Leland D.	TM3c
Fromiller, Karl J.	S1c
Fry, Clyde C.	SC1c
Furman, Phillip A.	CMoMM
Green, Wayne S. II	RT2c
Gunderson, Edwin Jr.	S1c
Hilgendorf, Donald R.	S1c
Hutchinson, Morris	EM2c
Jacobson, Gerald C.	S1c
Johnson, Charles H.	YM1c
Johnson, Russell L.	TM3c
Kalamen, Paul	CEM
Killough, Walter J.	CMoMM
Klosterman, Clarence J.	S1c
Kurtz, Leslie R.	Bkr3c
Langkil, Lawrence L.	MoMM3c
La Beuf, Alfred W.	RT3c
Lefler, Kenneth C.	SM2c
Levine, David H.	SM1c
Lister, William E.	RM2c
Lund, Paul E.	RM3c
Maledy, Kenneth L.	F1c
McFadden, Ralph W.	PhM1c
McKay, Claude J.	StM1c
Medlock, Charles H.	MoMM3c
Mossing, William F.	MoMM2c
Nielson, Russell H.	MoMM2c
Olson, Carroll A.	F2c
Pisarczyk, Frank	MoMM2c

Powell, Frederick E.	F1c
Ring, Herbert Jr.	S1c
Schechter, Charles	MoMM3c
Schmidt, David	S1c
Shackelford, Theodore E.	CTM
Seyfert, Edward K.	F1c
Steele, Creinghton S.	MoMM1c
Sturr, Thomas Jr.	MoMM1c
Tacke, Milton C.	RM3c
Talbot Verne M.	MoMM2c
Telthorst, Vernon L.	EM3c
Tomaselli, Jake	EM2c
Walker, Keefe	EM1c
Walsh, Thomas E.	EM2c
Watt, James B.	EM3c
Wheeler, Hubert	EM3c
Williamson, Phillip L.	TM2c
Wright, James D.	EM2c
Yanik, William P.	F1c
Zimmerman, Robert C.	SM2c

Ten Officers and Seventy Two Enlisted

Other Crew Members that received medals:

Adams, O. B.	Ltjg	Bronze Star
Armstrong, Kenneth G.	EM1c	Bronze Star
Johnson, W. H.	Lt	Silver Star
Roach, D. F.	Ltjg	Navy Commendation

Submarine service is all volunteer and each man undergoes psychological testing to insure he is just slightly crazy enough to do live in a sewer pipe and another trait is they must be easily amused and entertained; they must also be inventive. An excellent example comes from the USS Barb's twelfth patrol. By this time in the war targets for the submarines are getting hard to find, they have sunk almost all of the enemy's shipping, so they were getting bored. A bored submarine crew is dangerous. They spotted a train track with lots of traffic a mile inland from the coast of Japan and decided this would be an interesting diversion. On 23 July 1945

eight crewman (one from each department) rowed ashore in rubber rafts, hiked a mile inland and planted a scuttling charge under the tracks with a contact exploder they had made. On the way back to the boat, a train hit it and blew up. They got credit for sinking a train. They were the only U.S. servicemen to set foot on the island of Japan during the war. Watch out for bored submariners. For more amusing adventures of the USS Barb read the book Thunder Below by Admiral Eugene B. Fluckey, another remarkable submarine skipper.

FOURTEENTH PATROL

What would have been the **Fourteenth Patrol**

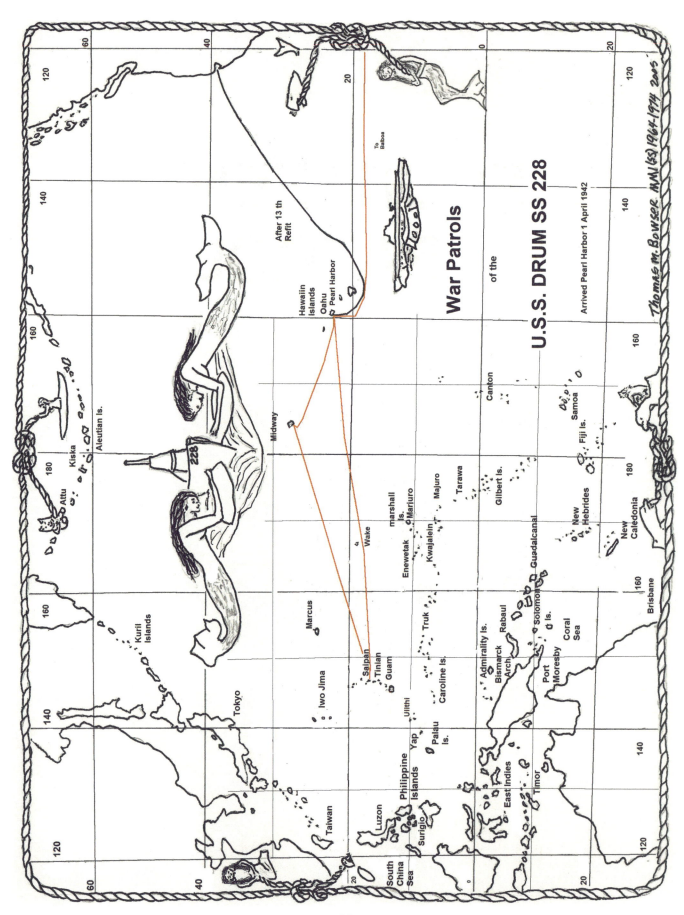

What was to be Drum's 14th Patrol was not documented with a patrol report because the war ended before she got on station. The following account has been pieced together from various records found on board the Drum in February 2009.

Commanding Officer: LCdr Eddy

26 June-10 July 1945 Sea trials and a dry docking
11 July Left Hunters point San Francisco for Pearl harbor
20 July Arrived Pearl Harbor
21 July Left Pearl Harbor for Midway
26 July Arrived Midway
27 July-8 August Training around Midway including a dry docking
11 August Left Midway for Saipan
!6 August Received radio message announcing Japans surrender
18 August Arrived Saipan
19 August Left Saipan for Pearl Harbor
30 August Arrived Pearl Harbor
31 August Left Pearl Harbor for Balboa at Panama Canal
16 September Arrived Balboa
17 September Left Balboa thru the Canal for New York
23 September (approximate) Arrived New York at Staten Island
25 September Left New York for Portsmouth N.H.
24 October Left Portsmouth for Boston
31 October Left Boston for Newport, Rhode Island
1 November Left Newport for New London, Connecticut

Due to the long refit at Hunters Point and the fact that Drum had 13 new crew members and much new equipment, they had the 11 day training at Midway. If Drum had arrived at Saipan just three days sooner this would have counted as the 14th Patrol. The stops at Pearl Harbor and Balboa were for refueling, they weren't wasting any time getting home.

The Crew members listed here reported aboard the Drum some time during the 1945 overhaul at Hunters Point or later and rode the boat on what would have been the 14th Patrol. They took the boat from Hunters Point to Pearl Harbor, to Midway, to Saipan, back to Pearl, to Balboa in the Canal Zone, to New York, Boston, Newport, R.I., and New London.

Archer, G. R.	TM3	Hagman, A. E.	MoMM2	Lopez, N. M.	RM3
Brewer, E. G.	YM2	Hiss, W. F.	MoMM1	McCann, J. J.	Ltjg
Butcher, E. C.	MoMM2	Henson, R. A.	MoMM1	Madlich, C. H.	MoMM3
Brock, C. R.	F1c	Hill, J. G.	TM2	Maxwell, Gainey S.	GM3
Brown, H. R.	STm2	Hahn, H. J.	MoMM1	McNeal, H. P.	LCdr
Carlson, A. F.	S1c	Jackson, N.	RM1	Mitchell, W. T.	YM1
Chandler, P. J.	S1c	Johnson, E.	S1c	Niles, T. E.	CTM
Cizer, C. S.	EM2	Krivacic, P. J.	ETm2	Navine, A. H.	F1c
Callahan, T. C.	CMoMM	Lander, L. W.	MoMM3	Paridise, H. W.	GM2
Ellis, D. C.	YM3	Ladd, G. E.	QM3	Robinson, D.	SC1
Foxworth, L. C.	TM2	Likkie, R.	TM3	Snyder, H. W.	Ens
Groundry, R. L.	S1c	Lieb, J. A.	F1c	Sidebottom, C. W.	TM1
Greenler, D.W.	F1c	Lomax, G. F.	STm1	Villani, P. J.	EM2
				Wilson, R. K.	CPHm

Because this was not an official war patrol we do not have a sailing list. The above list was compiled from the list of men transferred off the Drum at decommissioning that was found on board. Although the war was over the Drum was at hazard for the almost three month voyage, our submarines were still being attacked for several days after the end and we were never safe from our own forces and from collisions. The Drum had a fire in Maneuvering room off of South Carolina that was very serious and could have been disastrous and that is why the list above is included.

Some items of interest:

The first crew ashore in New York was Stateside. As they were pulling in Stateside spotted a female dog in the crowd welcoming them home and jumped ashore, the crew was able to get him back.

We found three letters from a bakery in Massachusetts requesting the payment that was owed them for the delivery of some pastries to the Drum, the amount owed was one dollar. If anyone from the Bakery reads this, I will be happy to pay the bill, but no interest.

The WWII Crew

Name	Rate	Patrols	14th	Total
Abell, William K.	S1c	11		1
Adams, O. B.	Ens	8, 9, 10, 11, 12, 13	X	6
Alamia, Anthony J.	F2c	1, 2, 3, 4, 5, 6		5
Allen, Frank L.	F2c	6, 7, 8, 9		4
Anderson, Gilbert M.	S2c	2, 3, 4, 5		4
Anderson, Robert L.	EM3c	1, 2, 3, 4, 5, 6, 7, 8, 9		9
Applegate, Elvin C.	TM2c	1, 2, 3, 4, 5, 6, 7, 8, 9, 10		10
Armstrong, Kenneth G.	EM1c	1, 2, 3, 4, 5, 6		6
Bader, G. H.	Ens	11, 12, 13		3
Baker, James E.	F1c	9, 10, 11, 12, 13		5
Baker, Nesbert D.	AB, S2c	1, 2, 3, 4, 5, 6		6
Barnett, George M.	F1c	12, 13		2
Barrell, David C.	EM1c	1, 2, 3		3
Bell, Edgar A	F1c, MM2c	1, 2, 3, 4, 5, 6, 8		7
Birdsell, Donald A.	RM3c	11, 12, 13	X	3
Bledsoe, James E.	S1c	10, 11, 12, 13	X	4
Bloom, William	StM2c	12, 13		2
Boap, Emmett J.	TM1c	11, 12,13	X	3
Boldt, Charles W.	F2c	6, 7, 8, 9		4
Brown, James C.	S1c	9, 10, 11, 12, 13		5
Brownell, Ralph E.	MoMM2c	5, 6, 8		3
Buckbee, William D.	EM2c, MM2c	1, 2, 3, 4		4
Bundy, John T.	MM2c	2, 4, 5		3
Burke, John A.	EM3c	1, 2, 3, 4, 5, 6, 7, 8		8
Bourland, James H.	AS	3		1
Campbell, Robert M.	TM2c	12, 13	X	2
Carmean, Myrlon H.	S2c, TM1c	2, 3, 4, 5, 6, 8, 9, 10, 11, 12		10
Carr, Roy	TM2	4, 5, 6, 7, 8, 9		6
Caverly, John E.	MM2c	1, 2, 3		3
Caviness, Daniel D.	RM2c	1, 3		2
Champion, James R.	S1c	11, 12, 13	X	3
Chase, Carl C. jr	S2c	2, 3		2
Chico, Dominick P	S1c	9, 10, 11, 12, 13		5
Chipman, Hubert H.	F1c	12, 13	X	2
Cleveland, Edward C.	MM1c	1, 2, 3		3
Cole, Percy	RM2c	12, 13		2
Connolly, P. J.	Ens	11, 12, 13	X	3
Conyers, Milton E.	TM2c	1, 2, 3		3
Corbett, Glenn O.	EM3c	6, 7		2
Cox				
Cozier, Charles S.	RM3c	10, 11, 12, 13		4
Criswell, Lane P.	YM1	2, 3		2
Crowe, Ray A.	Momm2c	10, 11, 12, 13	X	4

Name	Rate	Patrols	X	Count
Crowe, Audle L.	GM1c	1, 2, 3, 4, 5, 6, 7, 8, 9		9
Curtis, Warren G.	SM2c	7		1
Custer, Joseph W. Jr.	S1c	13	X	1
Dalwitz, Wilbert W.	AS, S2c	1, 2, 3, 5, 6		5
Dawson, Elijah jr	MAtt2c	2, 3, 4, 5, 7, 8		6
Decoo, George F. Jr.	YM1c	6, 7, 8		3
DeGrazio, Tony	CSM	4, 5 ,6, 7, 8, 9, 10		7
Deighan, Walter F.	S2c	2		1
DeRosa, Gerard J.	Bkr3c	6, 7, 8, 9, 10		5
Dial, Harrel	RT2c	4		1
Dittmeyer, Jack L.	RM1c	11, 12, 13		3
Dixon, Donald T.	S1c	9, 10		2
Dodd, Oliver L.	SC3c	12, 13		2
Doran, Hugh J. III	FCS2c	10, 11, 12, 13		4
Dozier, Henry H.	MM2c	1, 2, 3, 4, 5, 6, 7		7
Dunphy, Joseph L.	MoMM1c	13	X	1
Dye, Ira	Ltjg	3, 4		2
Dzik, Edwars H.	SC2c	1, 2, 3		3
Echols, Albert L.	GM3c	13		1
Eddy, F. M.	LCdr	12, 13		2
Eksterowicz, Edward	F1c	5, 6, 7, 8, 9, 10		6
Elkins, William C.	GM3c	8, 9, 10, 11, 12	X	5
Eller, Dock M.	MM1c	1, 2, 3, 4, 5, 6, 7, 8		8
Etheridge, W. R.	Lt	12, 13		2
Eubanks, James W.	MoMM2c	4, 5, 6, 7, 8, 9, 10, 11, 12, 13		10
Fedor, Robert C.	EM3c	4, 5, 6		3
Fellow, Everett N.	SC1c	7		1
Ferguson, Donald I.	S1c	1		1
Fischer, Arthur C.	TM2c	13	X	1
Fleischman, Russell	S1c	13		1
Flynn, Thomas Jr.	S2c	1		1
Fooks, Raymond	F1c	10, 11		2
Fox, Conrad L.	EM1c	5, 6, 7, 8, 9, 10, 11, 12		8
Foxworthy, Leland D.	TM3c	9, 10, 11, 12, 13		5
Fromiller, Karl J.	S1c	13		1
Frederick, Clayton J.	EM3c	9, 10, 11		3
Fry, Clyde C.	SC2c	9, 10, 11, 12,13		5
Furman, Phillip A.	CMoMM	9, 10, 11, 12, 13		5
Galas, Alexander	SM3c	1, 4, 5, 6		4
Ganley, John F. Jr	MM1c	1, 2		2
Getzewich, Julian	MM1c	1		1
Green, Wayne S. II	RT1c	10, 11, 12, 13		4
Gunderson, Edwin Jr.	S1c	13	X	1
Gurganus, Arthur A.	CTM(AA)	1, 2, 3		3
Habermehl, Bernard J.	F1c	1		1
Haines, Orval G.	CPhM	1, 2, 3, 4, 5		5

Name	Rank	Patrols		Count
Hanks, William E.	Ltjg	7, 8, 9, 10, 11		5
Hardin, "E" "M"	AS	1		1
Harper, John D	Ens	1, 2, 3, 4, 5, 6		6
Harris, Celeb S.	SC3c	6, 7		2
Harris, Charles E.	TM2c	1, 3		2
Havens, Paul G.	SC1c	3, 4, 5		3
Hazapis, T.	Ens	5, 6, 7, 8, 9, 10		6
Helgerson, Joseph	S2c	1, 2, 3, 4, 5, 6, 7, 8, 9, 10		10
Heller, Jack E.	EM1c	4, 5, 6, 7		4
Henderson, Lee R,	Sc2	6, 7, 8		3
Hilgendorf, Donald R.	S1c	13	X	1
Hudson, John E.	S1c	7, 8, 9		3
Hutchison, Jack M.	EM2c	10, 11, 12, 13	X	4
Ireland, Joe N.	RM2c	4, 5, 6, 7		4
Jacobson, Gerald C.	S1c	10, 11, 12, 13		4
James, Willie	MAtt3c	1		1
Jewell, Conrad D.	TM3c	1		1
Johnson, Charles C.	YM1c	9, 10, 11, 12, 13		5
Johnson, Charles H.	S2c	7, 8		2
Johnson, Leonard M.	S1c	5		1
Johnson, Russell L.	TM3c	7, 8, 9, 10, 11, 12, 13		7
Johnson, W. H.	Lt	10, 11, 12, 13	X	4
Jones, Arthur	S1c	7		1
Jones, Harry	RM2c	8, 9, 10		3
Kalamen, Paul	CEM	9, 10, 11, 12, 13		5
Kane, Thomas P. Jr.	TM3c	4, 5, 6, 7, 8		5
Kash, Arthur	AS	2, 3, 4, 5, 6, 7, 8, 9, 10, 11, 12		11
Kearns, Glenn E.	S2c	4, 5, 6, 7		4
Kellett, George W.	SC1c	9, 10, 11		3
Kelly, R. O.	Ens	4, 5		2
Kess, Samuel S.	F1c	1, 3, 4		3
Killough, Walter J.	CMoMM	9, 10, 11, 12, 13		5
Kimmel, Manning M.	Lt	1, 2, 3, 4		4
Kissinger, Robert	TM2c	6, 7, 8, 9, 10, 11		6
Klosterman, Clarence Jr.	S1c	11, 12, 13		3
Korte, E, J.	Ens	13	X	1
Kronholm, Donald E.	S1c	8, 9, 10, 11, 12		5
Krooner, Edward W.	MM2c	1, 3, 4, 5, 6, 7		6
Kuhn, Marvin G.	S2c	3, 4, 5		3
Kurtz, Leslie R.	SC3c	11, 12		2
La Beuf, Alfred W.	RT3c	9, 10, 11, 12, 13	X	5
La Mark Christopher P.	S1c	1, 2, 3		3
Lamfers, Albert W.	TM3c	6, 7, 8, 9, 10, 11		6
Lang, Emerson C.	F1c	1, 2, 5, 6, 7, 8, 9		7
Langkill, Lawrence L.	MoMM2c	8, 9, 10, 11, 12, 13	X	6
Lazo, Edward	S1c	9, 10		2

Name	Rate	Patrols		Count
Leach, Gilbert E.	F1c	1, 2, 3, 4, 5, 6, 7, 8, 9		9
Lefler, Kenneth C.	SM2c	11, 12, 13	X	3
Lehman, Roland E.	TM2c	1, 2		2
Levine, David H.	SM1c	12, 13	X	2
Lindsay, Robert G. Jr	RM3c	2, 4, 5		3
Lister, William E.	RM2c	9, 10 ,11, 12, 13		5
Lund, Paul E.	EM3c	11, 12, 13	X	3
Lytle, George W.	MAtt1c	1, 2, 3, 4, 5, 6, 7, 8, 9, 10, 11		11
Macarelli, Joseph S.	F2c	6, 7, 8		3
Maledy, Kenneth L.	F1c	11, 12, 13		3
Manning, Robert L.	CMM	1		1
Martin, Armor W.	F3c	1, 2, 3, 4		4
Martin, Sidney J.	QM1c	1, 2, 3, 4		4
May, Maynard D.	PhM1c	6, 7, 8		3
Mossing, William F.	MoMM2c	9, 10, 11, 12, 13		5
McClendon, William H.	SM1c	1, 2, 3		3
McCowan, James L.	TM3c	6, 7, 8		3
McFadden, Jack L.	F3c	4		1
McFadden, Ralph W.	PhM1c	9, 10, 11, 12, 13		5
McIntire, Kenneth E.	S1c	7		1
McKay, Claude J.	StM1c	9, 10, 11, 12, 13		5
McKinney, Samuel W.	F2c	1, 2, 3, 4, 5		5
McMahon, Bernard F	LCdr	4, 5, 6, 7		4
Medlock, Charles H	MoMM3c	13		1
Meyer, John J.	TM2c	6, 8, 9, 10		4
Morgan, Ernest L.	CEM	1		1
Mullen, John T.	Em3c	10, 11		2
Murphy, Arthur C.	EM3c, EM2c	1, 2		2
Nelson, R. E.	Lt	10, 11, 12, 13		4
Nichols, Harvey E.	S2c	3, 4, 5		3
Nicholas, Nicholas J.	Lt	1, 2, 4		3
Nielson, Russell H.	MoMM2c	10, 11, 12, 13		4
Olson, Carroll A.	F2c	10, 11, 12, 13		4
Olson, Robert L.	YM2c	4		1
Otto, Delbert R.	MM1c	1, 2, 3, 4		4
Owens, Hardy B.	CMoMM	6, 7, 8		3
Parker, Charles W.	S1c	3, 4, 5		3
Pepper, Ruben H.	CEM	1, 2, 3		3
Peterson, William J.	AS	2, 3, 4, 5		4
Pettigrew, Rex L.	F3c	3, 4, 5, 6		4
Phillips, Rollie P.	TM2c	5, 6, 7, 8, 9, 10, 11, 12		8
Pisarczyk, Frank	MoMM2c	7, 8, 9, 10, 11, 12, 13		7
Powell, Frederick E.	F1c	11, 12, 13	X	3
Pridonoff, Eugene	Ens	2, 3, 4, 5, 6, 7, 8, 9, 10, 11, 12		11
Psencik, Robert L.	MM1c	1, 3		2
Pyle, Clarence L.	TM1c	1, 2, 3, 4, 5, 6, 7, 8		8

Name	Rank	Patrols	X	Total
Ramsing, Verner U.	Ens	1, 2, 3, 4, 5, 6, 7, 8, 9		9
Reed, Gordon M.	AS	2, 5, 6		3
Rice, Robert H.	LCdr	1, 2, 3		3
Rich, Jack M.	F2c, F1c	1, 2, 3, 4, 5, 6, 7, 8, 9, 10, 11		11
Rindskopf, Maurice H.	LCdr	1, 2, 3, 4, 5, 6, 7, 8, 9, 10, 11		11
Ring, Herbert Jr.	S1c	12, 13	X	2
Ritchie, Robert W.	F1c	3, 4, 5, 6		4
Roach, D. F.	Ltjg	9, 10, 11, 12, 13		5
Robbins, Jack R.	EM1c	8, 9, 10		3
Rodgers, Charles	S2c	9		1
Rogers, John D.	EM2c	1		1
Rosset, Waldo D.	EM3c	1, 2, 3, 4		4
Rowe, James E.	S2c	5, 6		2
Royal, Arthur J.	StM1c	6		1
Ruebush, Calvin B.	TM3c	5, 6, 7, 8, 9, 10, 11, 12		8
Ryan, Joseph E.	MM1c	1, 2, 3, 4, 5		5
Ryan, L. L.	Ens	13		1
Satterwhite, Marshall	TM2c	1, 2, 3, 4		4
Savage, Carl H.	S1c	3		1
Shackelford, Theodore E.	CTM	12, 13		2
Schaedler, George A.	EM1c	3, 4, 5, 6, 7, 8, 9		7
Schechter, Charles	MoMM3c	12, 13	X	2
Scheiking, Walter D.	F2c	8		1
Schmidt, David	S1c	12, 13	X	2
Serrand, Angelo A.	F1c	8		1
Seyfert, Edward K.	F1c	13		1
Shonerd, W.	Ens	11		1
Simko, Frank M.	AS	2, 4, 5, 6, 7, 8, 9, 10, 11, 12		10
Simmons, Charles G. jr	S2c	2, 3		2
Simpson, Clyde R.	AS	2		1
Smith, Alvah P. Jr.	EM1c	5, 6, 7, 8, 9, 10, 11		7
Smith, Andrew J.	GM2c	6		1
Smith, Walter L.	S2c	1		1
Sponseller, Howard L.	TM1c	1, 2		2
Stafford, Archie D.	S1c	2		1
Steele, Creighton S.	MoMM1c	9, 10, 11, 12, 13	X	5
Stempf, Charles R.	Ltjg	8, 9, 10, 11, 12		5
Stockton, Charles E.	TM3c	3, 4, 5		3
Stout, Claude G.	CEM	9, 10		2
Straight, John E.	F2c	6, 7		2
Stilson, Louis A.	F3c	4		1
Stover, Rual C.	S1c	4, 5, 6		3
Sturr, Thomas Jr.	MoMM1c	12, 13		2
Style, Norman V.	RM3c	3, 4, 5, 6		4
Sullenger, James M.	FC1c	1, 2, 3, 4, 5, 6, 7, 8, 9, 10		10
Swarts, Richard	YM1c	1		1

Name	Rate	Patrols		Count
Swope, William R.	RM2c	6, 7, 8, 9, 10, 11		6
Szymanski, Ted	AS	2, 3, 5, 6, 7, 8, 9		7
Tacke, Milton C.	RM3c	11, 12, 13	X	3
Talbot, Verne M.	MoMM2c	7, 8, 9, 11, 12, 13		6
Telthorst, Vernon L.	GM3c	12, 13		2
Thibideau, Ronald W.	EM3c	7, 8, 9		3
Tomaselli, Jake	EM2c	8, 9, 10, 11, 12, 13		6
Truxton, Joseph J.	F3c	3, 4		2
Valenzuela, Edward T.	MoMM1c	10, 11		2
Vaughan, Donald O.	RM3c	1, 2, 3, 4, 5, 6, 7		7
Vaughan, Richard H.	S2c	2		1
Wajda, Steve J.	F3c	2, 3, 4, 5, 7, 8, 9, 10, 11		9
Walker, Keefe	EM1c	13		1
Walsh, Edward F.	SC1c	1, 2		2
Walsh, Thomas E.	EM2c	9, 10, 11, 12, 13		5
Watson, James D.	SM1c	5, 6, 7, 8, 9, 10, 11, 12		8
Watt, James B.	EM3c	10, 11, 12, 13	X	4
Waycasey, William E.	MoMM2c	3, 4		2
Webber, James F.	MoMM1c	6, 7, 8		3
Wentz, Royce E.	S1c	1, 2, 3, 4, 5, 6, 7, 8, 9,10,11,12		12
West, Thomas H.	S2c	3, 4		2
Wheeler, Hubert	EM3c	10, 11, 12, 13	X	4
White, Raymond F.	TM2c	6, 7		2
White, Robert E.	F3c	2, 3, 4, 5, 6, 7, 8, 9, 10, 11, 12		11
Whitright, Earl B.	EM3c	1, 2, 3, 4, 5 ,6, 7, 8, 9		9
Wilkinson, Edward N.	RM1	1, 2		2
Williamson, D. F.	Cdr	8, 9		2
Williamson, Phillip L.	S1c	3, 4, 5, 7, 8, 9, 10, 11, 12, 13		10
Wolf, William H.	S2c	3, 4, 5, 8		4
Workman, Thomas M.	TM1c	4, 5, 6, 9, 10, 11		6
Wright, James D.	EM2c	9, 10, 11, 12, 13		5
Wright, Lowell S.	MM2c	1, 2, 5		3
York, Keith L.	S1c	1, 2		2
Young, C. M.	Lt	6, 7, 8, 9, 10, 11, 12		7
Yanik, William P.	F1c	12, 13	X	2
Zimmerman, Robert C.	SM2c	9, 10, 11, 12, 13		5

The following men may have been aboard for what would have been the fourteenth patrol

Archer, G. R.	TM3
Brewer, E. G.	YM2
Butcher, E. C.	MoMM2c
Brock, C. R.	F1c
Brown, H. R.	STm2
Carlson, A. F.	S1c

Chandler, P. J.	S1c
Cizier, C. S.	EM2c
Callhan, T. C.	CMoMM
Ellis, D. C.	YM3
Foxworth, L.C.	TM2c
Groundrey, R. L.	S1c
Greenler, D. W.	F1c
Hagman, A. E.	MoMM2c
Hiss, W. F.	MoMM1c
Henson, R.A.	MoMM1c
Hill, J.G.	TM2
Hahn, H. J.	MoMM1c
Jackson, N.	RM1
Johnson, E.	S1c
Krivacic, P. J.	ETm2c
Lander, L. W.	MoMM3
Ladd, G. E.	QM3
Likkle, R.	Tm3c
Leib, J. A.	F1c
Lomax, G. F.	STm1c
Lopez, N. M.	RM3
McCann, J. J.	Ltjg
Madlich, C. H.	MoMM3
Maxwell, Gainey S.	GM3
McNeal, H. P.	LCdr
Mitchell, W. T.	YM1
Niles, T. E.	CTM
Navine, A. H.	F1c
Paridise, H. W.	Gm2c
Robinson, D.	SC1
Snyder, H. W.	Ens
Sidebottom, C.W.	TM1c
Villani, P. J.	EM2
Wilson, R. K.	CPHm

The Second Life

The Reserve Period

The Drum was decommissioned in February 1946 and re-commissioned in February 1947 to be used as a reserve training boat in Washington, D. C. at the Washington Navy Yard. She would not go to sea again under her own power but continued to serve with honor up until 1967 when she was finally retired and sent to the reserve fleet in Norfolk, Va. In 1969 she was towed to Mobile, Al to join the Battleship Memorial Park and to become the first submarine to be opened for public display.

During this time as a training boat, the reserves removed a lot of equipment to make room for class rooms (see the restoration chapter) and the propellers and batteries were removed. Thankfully most of it was left on board and stowed under the forward torpedo room deck, in after battery and the cool room. Little is known about this time period except for what is in the machinery history records which were kept up until around 1958, and what we have learned from submarine veterans that either trained on her or were assigned as crew (one of which was later a shipmate of mine on the Nuclear missile submarine USS James Madison SSBN-627, Jimmie Johnson MM1 (SS), an A-ganger). We would appreciate hearing from anyone that has information or stories about the Drum from this period.

During all the war patrols the Drum never lost a crewman, which was pretty unusual for submarines during the war, and she was known as a happy and lucky boat.

In April 2012, at the South East Regional Conference of the United States Submarine Veterans, I was told of the death of a crewman on the Drum by one of the Sub Vets who served on her in the fifties. He did not have a name or the year but said someone had died in #1 Main ballast tank and we have not been able to find anything about it.

On July 3rd I received an email from Bill Jordan who said his father (James Franklin Jordan TMC) had died on the Drum on 25 July 1952 and he and his family would like to come to the boat for the 60th anniversary of his death.

Frank joined the Navy in 1939 and served on the USS Louisville CA-28 and they may have witnessed the British capture of the German Battleship Graf Spree in Uruguay. They then went to Africa to pick up 148 million in gold from the British to transport back to the U.S. for safe keeping. The Louisville was on its way from Borneo to Pearl Harbor on 7 December 1941.

Frank completed submarine school on 23 June 1941 and served on the USS Mackerel SS-204 and then was assigned to the USS Queenfish SS-393 and made all five of her patrols. The Queenfish was credited with sinking 8 ships for about 40,000 tons, a very good record for a boat coming late into the war when targets were getting hard to find. When Queenfish ended the war she was sent to San Diego and Frank returned to New London and went to the Spikefish SS-404 and then to the USS Drum SS-228.

According to the machinery history records the crew of the Drum was servicing the ballast tank flood ports and operating gear during July 1952. Frank and some of his shipmates were leaving the boat for liberty and Frank saw that the hatch for #1 MBT was still open in the forward torpedo room. Frank was a torpedo man and probably concerned for the safety of his shipmates, told the others to go ahead and get the car and he would catch up with them on the pier. It is not known how Frank ended up in the tank, but when he didn't show up his shipmates came back looking for him and found him in the #1 MBT, he had already succumbed from lack of oxygen.

It is tragic that Frank survived the whole war and then died in this manner. He gave his life in true submarine tradition of looking out for his shipmates and he will be remembered for this. Frank is on eternal patrol with many of his shipmates.

Sailor, rest your oar

It was later learned that Frank had broken his neck while on liberty diving into a lake a year before and it is hypothesized that the strain from trying to close the hatch to the tank may have caused him to black out and fall into the tank.

In June of 2008 the movie crew for the movie USS Seaviper came to shoot a trailer for the movie. They were getting ready to shoot in the forward engine room and had it all fogged up. Just before they turned on the camera, there was a swirl of fog through the aft door like someone just walked through it. Who knows?

The Third Life

The Restoration Crew of the USS Drum SS 228

Tom Bowser
Submarine Veteran
Volunteer

Lesley Waters
Park employee

Restoration of the USS Drum
By Thomas M. Bowser MM1(SS)

There is so much more to the story of restoring the Drum than an account of time, money and effort spent. The real story is about two people. One, Lesley Waters, who is a dedicated employee of the Battleship Park, dedicated to the drum. It is her passion and drive to preserve and restore the Drum that first got me interested in the boat. It is a story of her frustration of working alone, doing the impossible with little or no hope of getting any help, of hearing promises from sub vets that never got filled, of the constant battle against time and visitors, trying to restore the inside of the boat, knowing all the while that the elements were winning on the outside and knowing that by herself there wasn't anything she could do but hope and keep working. The other person is myself. It is the story of how the two of us have taken on a project that no one else has considered doing and we are told almost every day that we are crazy and that two people can't do it. Yes we are crazy, but by starting with nothing and without help we are getting it done and we are getting help. When people hear about what we are doing and see us doing the impossible we get offers of help. Unfortunately we do not have the equipment to support physical help. When I tell companies of the time I am donating to this cause they willing give materials that I ask for and wonder how we are going to be able to do the job. We often look at each other and wonder ourselves how we are going to do it, but we look back and see what we have done and are amazed at how little time has passed and how much we have accomplished. Our greatest reward is the thanks from the sub vets that can't help us but would like to. It would be fantastic if somehow we could raise the money to hire out the work and to buy all the tools and material that we need, but we can't wait for it to rain money, I can't apply for grants as an individual so I had to find a way to get donations from people and other sources, more rusted areas are falling off. Along with not having the money we don't have the time either.

The story of the restoration of the Drum actually begins years ago. I got out of the Navy in August 1974 after having served aboard Nuclear Submarines and entered the world of the non-military. The next 26 years I spent going from job to job around the country, never thinking back on the submarine days but searching for something I couldn't put my finger on, something was missing and I couldn't find it.

In the year 2000 I was living in Enterprise, Al and had just taken a job as vendor for Lowes Home Improvement stores that required me to travel around the southeast. On one trip to the Mobile area I spotted a bill board that had the profile of a WWII submarine and the name USS Drum and that it was located at Battleship Memorial Park. After I had completed the work I was doing I stopped to see what it was about and found the USS Drum.

When I went down in the forward torpedo room the smell of the hydraulic oil and grease overwhelmed me and flooded my mind with the memories I had pushed to the back of my mind for all these years. I was completely overcome with emotions and had to sit down on the deck to recover. In a few minutes a lovely young lady came up and asked if I was all right, I just waved and nodded my head and she said, "oh you must be a sub vet, I will check back later". I had spent six weeks in 1965 on a diesel submarine, the USS Atule SS 403, while it was in the ship yard in Charleston, SC and while I was waiting for my first nuc boat to return from patrol, I did not remember much about it and it had been converted after the war so it was different than the Drum but after a bit I started to recognize systems and valves and other equipment. Lesley Waters, the lady that checked on me when I came aboard, gave me a tour of the boat and explained what her job was maintaining the boat. I think I got to go back to the boat one more time just before they took it out of the water and put it on land in 2001 and then I had to wait forever before I could get back to her.

During the years 2001 and 2002 I got back to the Drum on occasion and got to know more about her and Lesley and I became greatly impressed with the job Lesley was doing and her passion for the boat, how hard she was working and how much restoration she had already done, and it was during this time that I decided I needed to help her and the boat. I started by donating a set of tools to her and then I would bring supplies and more tools to make her job easier and I changed jobs and went to work for a vendor company that would eventually bring me past the boat every other week. From around February 2003 to April 2006 I visited the boat every chance I could which was usually every other week for a few hours on Mondays and most of Friday. I started helping Lesley identify objects, at first mainly galley equipment, and explain how it was used and where and it was located, during this time I purchased a copy of the Fleet Submarine Manual on DVD and printed it out so Lesley could use it for a reference book.

I found out that when they took the Drum out of the water they had one person at a time sand blasting the boat and they wouldn't let them paint until the whole boat was blasted, which took over a month. Then they painted during the winter months with whatever paint they had even different types and they were painting over the rust. Within a few years there were bubbles in the paint and when I poked them with my knife water came out. I kept asking the park director what they were going to do and he finally told me they didn't have the money or man power to do anything due to Katrina and the repairs needed in the park and that they didn't have the blueprints so they couldn't do the repair work anyhow. He told me "it's your boat, keep me informed" and re-emphasized that they didn't have the money to spend on the Drum.

The first two years, 2006 and 2007, we worked on restoring the inside of the boat while I started raising the money to do the outside and get supplies, tools and material. The majority of the money would come from the submarine veterans around the country, from going on a few of the forums on the internet, going to the local sub vets base meetings, and getting a letter in the sub vet magazine. A lot of donations of money, tools and materials came from me giving tours to the visitors on the weekends. As we started on the outside and made progress it got easier to get donations. From 2006 to 2012 I raised approximately $55,000 in donations and another $30,000 in donated tools and materials, plus what I purchased myself, and put in about 20,000 hours of volunteer time. Each year I would get just enough to keep us busy for the year. The submarine veterans have been the greatest; I figured they would start running when they saw me coming but they didn't and just went ahead and got their wallets out knowing what I was after. The more we learned of her history, and especially after we found all the records, logs and invoices on the boat, the more I realized how import it is to preserve her. We started to get more of the WWII crew families that haven't been to the reunions or to the boat contacting us and coming to see the Drum and that has made it all worthwhile. It is the greatest experience to be able to show someone where their father or relative worked, slept and what they ate and it is even better when we can show them a log or invoice with their signature.

It was during the period while I was traveling as a vendor that Lesley stripped and painted the escape hatch and trunk in the forward torpedo room and painted the conning tower.
The escape trunk was really nasty with chipped paint and cork and rust underneath the cork. Lesley had to scrape and pry off all the old cork, scrape the rust off the hull of the trunk, chip the old paint off of all the piping and repaint it all. She was in there for month.

The conning tower took her over a month to scrape and

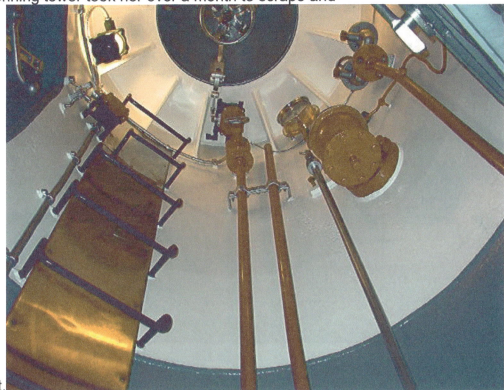

repaint.

Forward escape trunk

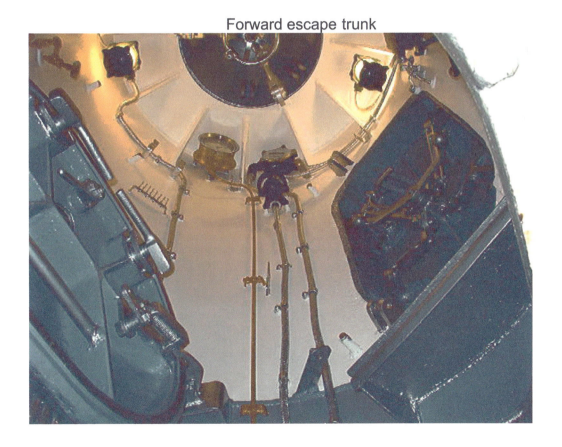

The Conning tower before Lesley painted and with the old periscope handles

Conning tower after painting

I also was able to attend my first crew reunion at this time and it was during this period that I discovered the internet and finally responded to a shipmate from one of my boats that had been trying to find me. Between the two I realized that I had found what I had been searching for ever since I got out of the Navy and that was the submarine family and I started to realize that I was a part of the Drum and it had been a major influence on my life before I was even born and I owed her for directing me to submarines.

In June 2005 I took a week's vacation to help Lesley get ready for the crew reunion and we stayed one night painting the interior deck until around midnight, it was great being on the boat at night with no visitors. The reunion was fantastic and I got to meet and talk with the crew, that was priceless.

Front row left to right-Donald Kronholm (Swede) patrols 8-12, Gerard DeRosa (Skinney Ghinney) 6-10, Eugene Pridonoff 2-12, George Schaedler 3-9, Tom Walsh 9-13, Alva Smith 5-11 Second row-Gainey Maxwell 14, Conrad Fox 5-12, Phillip Williamson (Willie) 3-13, Sammy Kess 1,3,4, Myrlon Carmean 2-12, Wayne Green 10-13

Crew reunion 2005

One of the first major discoveries was in the Refrigerator, when I finally got Lesley to open it. She had been told by the supervisors not to open or go into the closed spaces as they had been closed for many years. When we opened the refer hatch the first thing we saw was a huge radio right below the hatch with a lot of corrosion on it, but behind it I saw the foot of the food mixer. After a bit I went into the refer and looked at the mixer and saw it was buried underneath something else. I managed to move a few things around and worked the mixer closer to the ladder but had to leave and it was on another visit that we rounded up a come-along and hoisted the mixer out and put it on the deck in the galley. I picked up some paint and when I came back again Lesley had done one of her fantastic restoration jobs on the mixer and it looked like new. The next task was to figure out where it went and after looking around the galley we noticed the cut out in the bottom of the locker in back and checked the sink top and found holes that matched the mixer. We got the come-along out again and hoisted the mixer back to its home. We found the attachments in the dry food storage and Lesley cleaned those up.

The Food mixer before painting

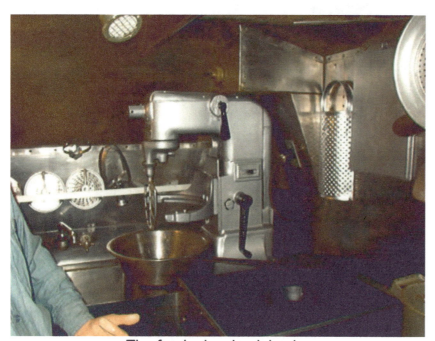
The food mixer back in place

In August of 2005 hurricane Katrina hit Mobile and the coast and shut down the park until January 2006. That was a long lonesome time, I felt like I had lost my best friend. In September 2005 while I was in Jacksonville, Florida for a James Madison reunion, I learned the company I was with had lost its contract and my job would be changing in a few months. Then in December my wife died. During this time I had been working on the tour guide and history book of the Drum and delivered them the week before it opened.

I had hoped that the gift shop would sell them at the ticket office window but later found out they wouldn't. I was only able to get to the Drum occasionally with the new job so I decided to move to get closer and in February I bought a 16' travel trailer and in March moved it to Enterprise, Alabama into my aircraft hanger. In March I interviewed with Home Depot in Daphne, AL. and then in April moved to Bay Minette.

We made many other minor discoveries over the next year or so, including the torpedo straps. In February of 2006 Lesley and I went to Galveston, Texas to see the Cavalla. It was a cold windy trip and we only spent an hour or so on the boat but found out our unknown torpedo pusher was for the Mark 18 electric torpedo and we managed to get the Cavalla's old periscope handles to replace the Drum's. We later sent some of the Drums torpedo straps to the Cavalla in exchange.

New periscope handles

After I moved to be close to the Drum and started working part time, I was able to be on the boat almost every day for at least four hours. In April 2006 we found the block and tackle in one of the forward tubes and a block of wood the right thickness under the deck and started restoring that. We repainted the control room and found a Mark 27 torpedo in the scrap pile, pulled it out and started on it.

The wood from the block and tackle

The block and tackle, it was used to retrieve practice torpedoes after the Drum fired them.

The control room water ways repainted, the bench lockers were in the refrigerator

In May I didn't get to the boat much due to work, but we continued work on the control room, the MK 27 and the block and tackle plus clean and polish for the Navy inspection.

I didn't know anything about the Mark 27 and when I researched it I found out they were the first electric homing torpedo developed in 1944 and were the first good torpedoes in the war. Just over 1,000 were made and the Drum carried them on the 13th patrol and we could only find 15 left. The Park had the torpedo on display outside until it started to rust and they threw it away.

The MK 27 torpedo as it was found

The MK 27 after restoration

In June we found the acey-deucey board in the mess table top and restored it, continued work on the block and tackle, got the ice cream machine out of the refer.. Then it was clean up and polish for the crew reunion and it was even better because I now knew some of the crew. After the reunion we placed the ice cream machine where the crew told us it went and then pulled the TBL radio out of the refer. This is a 600 lb. radio and I ended up getting three stitches in my brow when a chain link broke. A couple of days later we put the radio in the radio room where it belonged.

The Acey-Deuecy board restored

Crew reunion 2006

The ice cream machine

The half of the TBL Radio in the refrigerator

The TBL in radio after Lesley cleaned and painted

In July we continued to clean out the freezer and Lesley cleaned and painted the hydrogen detector we found, finished and hung the block and tackle and worked on the

MK 27. In July I quit Home Depot and started part time in the gift shop, big mistake and very disappointing. In August I moved to Spanish Fort to get closer to the boat because I wasn't making enough in the gift shop to stay where I was.

August-first part of November we stripped the hand rails using wire wheels on grinders and painted as we went along, we had help from the USS Kidd on a couple of occasions. This was not fun and didn't do a really good job but it was better than leaving them to rust for a few more years until we can sand blast them. In November we started cleaning the pump room, now this is fun. Last weekend in November I gave a tour to Ralph Villani, a movie producer whose father served on the Drum and he talked about doing a submarine adventure movie onboard the boat. We will see how this turns out.
We found the torpedo skid supports for the aft torpedo room in aft battery and started bringing them out.

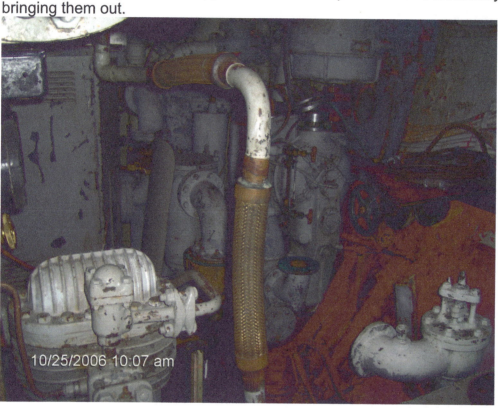

The pump Room before we started scrapping and painting

The Pump Room

It was about this time that I started giving tours on the boat after I was done in the gift shop. I would stay and talk to visitors until the park closed and sometimes much later. One of the first and longest tours was to Dan from Tennessee and the discussions are still going on five years later by email at least once a week, and he is my best contributor to the restoration. Another was Lance, who later became the web master for our web site www.drum228.org. Lance is from Mississippi and his uncle served on the USS Tambor during the war so I gave him the super tour and his website has been and still is the biggest help to us. I have met so many great people and given hundreds of tours; many of them come back each year to see our progress and this is one of the many things that keep us going.

Aft Torpedo Room skid supports

December 2006 we moved the barricade in the aft room and put the supports in place. Found the machinery history records and read them and then finally got the patrol reports and spent a few days reading them, what a trip back in time. The Drum has such a rich historic value, it is amazing. We finished moving and installing the skid supports and then moved one of the skids we found under the forward deck that had been cut in half, and then spliced it back together.

January 2007 we moved skids from under the deck to the deck of the forward torpedo room, started painting in the pump room and took down the photos on the crews mess bulkhead, removed the paneling and decided we were crazy. We then spent forever cleaning the adhesive and filling holes in the bulkhead and finally painted it.

Crew's Mess before

Aft bulkhead in crew's mess after removing paneling

After painting

February. We jumped back and forth on a lot of projects, another skid brought up out of the pit and hauled to the aft torpedo room, and Lesley cleaned and painted it and varnished the new blocks of wood we had to make for it. We started cleaning and painting the after port side of the pump room, now we are really having fun. We restored several small blocks we found and made a picture frame for the photos we took down in the crews mess and put the new picture frame in forward torpedo room. Lesley started painting the forward torpedo room outboard the skids on the port side.

Skids in Aft Torpedo Room

Pictures relocated from crews mess

March. We cleaned the forward torpedo room pit, painted in the pump room, finished painting forward torpedo room out board the skids and cleaned the tank tops under the deck. I finally got permission to weld and using my own 110v mig welder started repairing the aft topside deck.

April. We spent the whole month repairing the deck. I did the welding and Lesley wire brushed and painted.

May. We finished the deck repairs and cleaned up the boat inside and out for the Navy inspection which went real good, they were impressed with what we had accomplished and with our plan for the hull (well actually they said we were crazy, that two people couldn't rebuild a submarine with no money, we hear that a lot). After the inspection we got a small sand blaster and then started getting ready for the crew reunion.

June If I ever have any doubts that what I am doing is worthwhile they are completely erased at the crew reunions. The smiles and joy on their faces are all the reward I will ever need for the work I am doing. I hope that a hundred years from now a young person will be able to tell their friends "my great, great Grandfather served on this boat and this is where he worked and where he slept".

Front row L-R-Conrad Fox Patrols 5-12, ? , Phillip Williamson (Willie) 3-13, Wayne Green 10-13, Maurice Rindskopf 1-11, ? , Bob White 2-12, Tom Walsh 9-13, Alva Smith 5-11 Second row- Gainey Maxwell14, Myrlon Carmean 2-12, David Schmidt 12-13, Donald Kronholm (Swede) 8-12, Art Fisher13-14, George Schaedler 3-9

Crew reunion 2007

Admiral Mike Rindskopf in his stateroom, the last time he came aboard the Drum.

After the reunion we started working on the superstructure side on the starboard side. I would cut out rusted areas and weld in new metal that was donated by Sabel steel and Lesley would sand blast and paint. The sand blasting was very tedious, with a small blaster Lesley could only do about eight feet of aft structure before she had to stop due to visitors.

Sand blasting the starboard aft superstructure with our first small pot

Repair and sand blasting starboard super structure with a bigger pot

July-August Sand blast and paint and repair starboard superstructure. I went with one of the Park Commissioners to Oneal Steel in Mobile and they have agreed to donate all the steel to restore the boat.

September after a couple of weeks of superstructure work we were told to shut down because we were using all the air and the aircraft guy had to paint his airplanes. Lesley worked on the TBL radio while I was at work. We got a work party of 20 active duty chiefs from the USS Makin Island LHD-8 under construction in Pascagoula, MS and had them work on the sail and other areas. It surprised me but we got a lot of good work out of the chiefs. After the work party we finished up the sail, repaired the rail around the 40mm and painted them.

October while I made a heavy duty davit to assist us in loading equipment and supplies on to the boat, Lesley completed painting the sail and the 40mm gun. I then opened all the fuel tank access covers to inspect the inside of the tanks even though I was told by the maintenance people at the park I would not have to worry about them. It was as I suspected, all are rusted, not quite to the scale rust point but close. I found two completely full of water and we drilled holes in the bottom to drain them. We then moved inside and worked on #7 torpedo tube, and finally got the outer door open.

November we decided to move the racks (bunks) from the port bulkhead to the center in after battery so visitors would have a better idea of what it actually looked like. First we had to make new poles and hooks and then moved the racks. We met with Sherwin-Williams paint rep and they eventually agreed to donate paint to us. We than brought the MK 27 torpedo we had found in the scrap pile to the deck to restore it. We were told by the maintenance people we were wasting our time. We completed the MK 27 and moved it into the aft torpedo room after we removed the barricade. Lesley and Hal, one of our sub vet volunteers, painted the torpedo. The movie crew came at the end of the month to shoot a trailer for the WWII submarine adventure movie they are going to film on the Drum next year. The movie is called USS Seaviper and the director's father served on board during the war. We filmed at night and it was really interesting to watch them as they tried to set up their equipment in the various compartments. The Mark 27 we restored was the star of the aft torpedo room.

Removing locking wire from inboard exhaust valve forward engine room for the movie trailer. We didn't know at the time how much time we would spend on this and how long it would take.

Setting up in aft torpedo room. That is Ralph Villani on the left and Nick Schreoder on the right, Nick plays the Sonarman.

December we worked on the skid for the MK 27, making new wood blocks due to the size difference between the 27 and 14 torpedoes. We removed the old paneling from the port bulkhead in crews mess and Lesley started taking off the old adhesive.

Port bulkhead in crew's mess after removing paneling

Port bulkhead completed

January 2008 we worked on the 27, the Christmas tree in control and Lesley worked on sound powered phones. We brought a transformer on board and placed it under the sail on a shelf I had made for it. This will finally give us 220vac power to run a bigger welder. We tested the depth gages with air pressure and they all worked. As the depth gage was passing 100 feet I looked over and saw Lesley looking around and asked if she was looking for leaks, she said yes. In the middle of the month the movie crew and most of the actors came for a one night rehearsal. The actors were thrilled to be filming a movie on the boat and all were really interested in the history and what were are doing for the restoration. We then started cleaning up and fixing the torpedo firing panels in the conning tower.

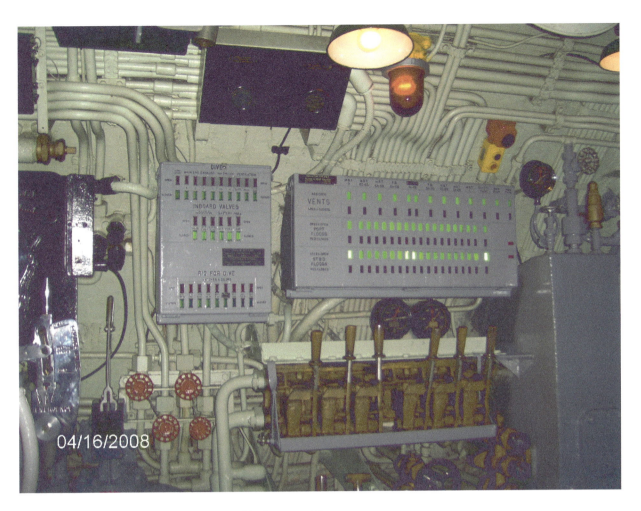

Christmas Tree

February. The first of February I quit working in the Gift shop so I could be on the Drum all day as a volunteer. During the first week we had volunteers from the USS Gettysburg CG-64, which was in Mobile for the Mardi Gras, for two days. We had them work on the bulkhead in crew's mess, painting in lower level aft engine room and aft torpedo room. It was the first time I had seen two Ensigns and a LTJG paint. The following week we had volunteers back from the Makin Island and had them help bury the conduit for our transformer, work on crew's mess bulkhead and paint aft torpedo room, and we moved the MK 27 from the forward room to the aft room. After the volunteers, I finished painting lower level engine room while Lesley finished cleaning the crews mess bulkhead, than we ran the wire and conduit for the 220 circuit. The sub vets and donations paid for the materials. We than made five new locker doors for the missing ones in crew's mess.

March. We finished running the 220 and 110 circuits with outlets under the deck topside, took the MK 27 back on deck to do some more work on it using the bigger welder, moved the 27 back below and installed straps on both torpedoes. We than painted the Christmas tree and repainted the lettering on the trees and inclinometer scales. Taking a break from the tedious work we explored inside and behind lockers in the galley. Lesley spotted some papers behind a pipe behind some drawers and they turned out to be letters sent to one of the cooks, Nesbert Baker, postmarked April and May 1942.

April. We had so much fun painting the lettering on the trees we decided to repaint the numbers and markings on the depth gages, now we are really having fun. Cleaned up the boat and got ready for Navy inspection which went off really good; one of the inspectors was here last year and he was amazed at what we had done. The last week of the month the movie people came back for nine nights of filming, 14-16 hours each night, talk about tired. The actors are really good and the movie is going to be great because it is real, being filmed in the boat and not a studio. The scenes filmed in the conning tower were really great, with four actors, the director, the cameraman and camera and all their extra lights, it was about 105 degrees and humid, very real.

Tim Large on the left (the Chief), Rob Maus (Capt. Culpepper), Myself as Me

Mike Tesch (special effects) Lesley, Me

May. The first week was filming the movie and then we rested and cleaned up the boat and put things back to normal. We made a platform to set our new air compressor on and then brought it on board and put it under the deck outboard the forward escape trunk. The compressor people came and did the initial startup and break in. We started working on the stern, I cut out some rusted areas and we found two feet of mud and sand under the torpedo tubes, so we cleaned that out along with all the loose rust. We started getting the boat ready for the crew reunion next month.

Starboard stern as we started, note small pot

June. The first week and a half is spent cleaning and polishing the old girl for the crew reunion. You can almost feel the boat quiver with anticipation of getting to see the men that rode her and brought her home from the war. The reunion was great, though sad because only 7 crewmen could make it and three families of departed crew. Two of the crew were in wheel chairs and couldn't get on the boat. Lesley and I went to their hotel each night to listen to their stories and to get answers to some questions we had. RalphVillani was there with a camera man and one of the actors and they recorded interviews of the crew for the documentary they are filming. On Thursday night I was able to announce that I had a professional sand blaster coming Monday morning to donate two days of work. The ceremony on Saturday was really great, the Makin Island had 16 crewmen in dress uniform in formation behind the podium and then they were side boys for the crew to go to the sea wall to throw flowers in the bay.

Front row L-R- David SchmidtPatrols 12-13, Eugene Pridonoff 2-12, Tom Walsh 9-13
Second row- Gainey Maxwell 14, Donald Kronholm (Swede) 8-12, Gerard DeRosa (Skinney Ghinney) 6-10, Bob White 2-12

Crew reunion with the Makin Island crew

Monday morning, 0600, the sandblaster (Sanco) arrived with his equipment and started work immediately on the starboard side of the hull. They blasted back to about the forward hatch and then primed working off of a ladder. Wednesday we got an air tank for our compressor and loaded it on board and under the deck at the forward escape trunk. Thursday the sandblaster returned and completed and primed back to between the 5" and the sail and then painted black on the first section. Finally, after two long years of struggle we are getting new black paint. It may not seem like much, but I can't begin to describe what a tremendous accomplishment this is.

After Sanco's first day

July through first two weeks of October

We completed repairs and sand blasting and painting of the starboard superstructure. We made a hoist frame to make it easier to raise, lower and move the scaffold and were able to raise our blasting capacity to 800 pounds of sand a day by starting at 0530 and working until visitors arrived. We used approximately 30 tons of sand.

Our hoist

October through December

For three weeks we worked on restoring the stern. We had to first go in between the torpedo tubes with a grinder and remove rust until we found solid enough metal to weld to and then start rebuilding the bottom partition back to where we could go up to support the top. The interior framing and partitions are almost complete and a new bottom piece is in and one side piece. The weather turned cold and damp and I had cataract surgery in both eyes in November and December and we both had bad colds.

Working at rebuilding the interior partition of the stern. There is very little room and sharp rusted edges everywhere..

Progress being made in the partition in the stern.

We got the outer torpedo tube door on tube 7 open and used the tube to store our welder and tools in at night.

Starboard stern

January and February 2009
We put up racks in the aft torpedo room on the starboard side to complete it, found the manual flare push rod and got the signal ejector working, found the blueprint for mounting the TBL and brought the second half out of after battery. We cleaned up the radio, made the mounting plate using the original casters and mounted both halves of the TBL in radio. We spent a week holding a major field day in the forward engine upper and lower. We found another acey-deuecy board on a crew's mess table and restored it.

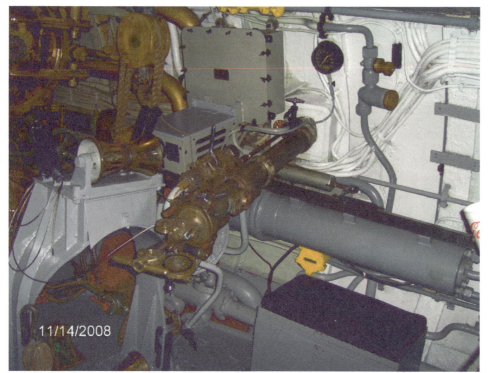

The Signal Ejector

The other half of the radio

The radio back together in radio

March
Brought up the crew's head partition and installed, the last item to be put back that the reserves had removed. Replaced bunk brackets with heavier ones. Removed inspection covers from periscope shears and radar masts, cleaned out rust and sand blasted and painted all. Replaced 6 inspection covers. Paint all water tight doors. Seaviper movie crew arrived on the 25th, started filming at night on the 26th.

The Seaviper film crew and some of the actors and extras from the USS Makin Island

Movie crew rest area in after torpedo room. Also make up room.

Movie control center in berthing on port side

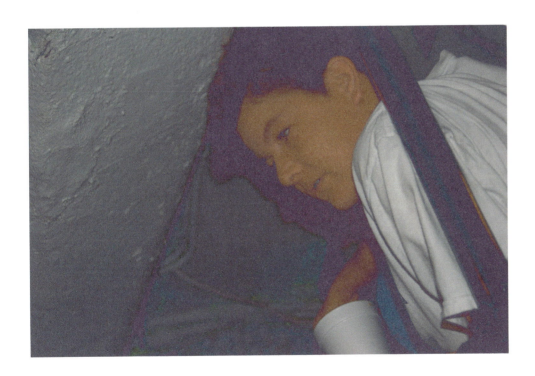

Lesley in the critic's gallery watching the monitor. We would stop them often to make corrections.
April
Seaviper finished filming on the 11th and left on the 12th, spent a week cleaning up the boat than back sand blasting and painting radar and 20mm.

May
Finish shears and 20mm. Finish interior and exterior starboard stern. Started sand blasting and painting starboard hull. We got the use of a 400# pot and large compressor from Sunbelt rentals and subvets rented a manlift.

The periscope shears after repairs and painting

June
Sand blast and paint starboard hull, continue welding stern and a break in the middle for the reunion. The crew was very happy to see the progress we are making on the boat, only had seven crew.

Lesley Waters, Phillip Williamson (Willie) patrols 3-13, Conrad Fox 5-12, Tom Bowser, Bob White 2-12, Donald Kronholm (Swede) 8-12, Art Fisher 13,14, David Schmidt 12, 13

Crew reunion 2009

Sand blasting the starboard hull. We had to sand blast between 5:30 am and 9:30 am to get it done before the visitors came over and then we would paint the primer on.

July
Finish welding on stern, sand blast and paint stern and starboard side. Mobile Mechanical loaned us an air compressor.

Back on the stern

Sand blasting starboard side

Starboard stern almost done, took creative metal bending

Starboard stern finished

August
Sand blasted and paint starboard hull and port bow and at new a/c platform. Finished starboard side except bottom. Started cleaning out rust from bow, made a bosun chair to do chain lockers and outboard tubes, removed #6 shutter door, found 6 feet of mud and rust, Lesley cleaned out bow while I knocked rust out of chain lockers and off hull, she had to use an air chisel to get the rust out.

Back to sand blasting

The starboard bow as we started on it

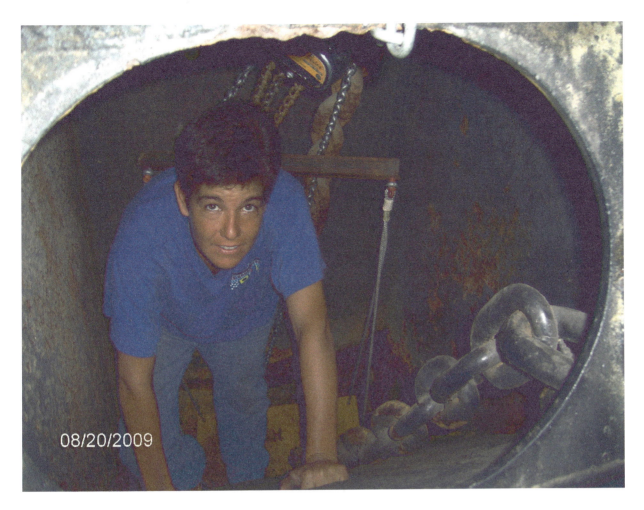

Lesley in the chain locker

September
Continued working on cleaning out bow and started welding new steel on hull. We are going to have to replace the bottom six feet on the starboard side and the bottom 10 feet of the interior and a few areas on the port side. Had the Historic Naval Ships conference in late September. It was really great to finally meet some of the other boat people. We also got to meet the Assistant Director from the Navy museum ship program. He told me that they had the Drum on the list to be considered for scrap because they knew the Park wasn't going to repair the boat and they had no hope that two crazy people with no money could do it. After showing him around and explaining how we were doing it, he said he was taking her off the scrap list.

Torpedo tube shutter door

Replacing interior framing inside bow

October and November
Continued work on the starboard bow including rebuilding partitions and framing inside, sand blasting inside and the shutter doors, rebuilding the two bottom shutter doors and rebuilding the hull around the torpedo doors. Lesley cut out new numbers (0, 1 and 2) with a torch and we welded those back on the hull. Sand blasted and painted starboard bow.

Rebuilding starboard bow, more creative metal bending. We used chain falls, pry bars, sledge hammers, ran over it with the fork lift and a few kind words.

Notice new numbers 0, 1, 2-Lesley cut those out of 1/8" steel

Starboard bow done

December
Moved inside for the winter. Redid some wiring to get heat in the after torpedo room, took down the battle flags from the sail and redid them.

January 2010
Finished battle flags, chipped and painted induction valves in crews mess, finished painting crews mess.

New Battle Flag

February
Started repainting officers country, we were going to do forward torpedo room but it was too cold. We painted in the passageway until visitors started coming in and then moved to the side rooms.

Three man stateroom repainted

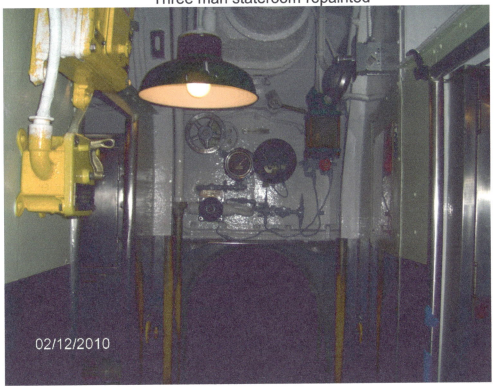

Forward Battery passageway

Forward Battery passageway looking aft

March
Finished painting officers country and moved topside again. Repairing after deck. Everywhere there is a frame the deck is rusting through because it was never sand blasted and painted. We are doing repair work now and will rebuild and sand blast the underside after we are done with the hull. Sometimes we feel like the rust is winning.

April
Continued working on deck and then superstructure, then repaired the Hunley replica. The last week we moved to the port side bow.

May
Rebuilt the port bow and doors. This time we left the doors in place and rebuilt around them to make it easier matching everything up. Sand blasted and painted port bow. Completed in three weeks, we are getting good. Moved to stern, made gate in fence for easier access and built scaffold.

This is the Port Bow showing six feet of mud and rust. The bottom torpedo tube door is completely buried, we almost cried when we saw this. Lesley cleaned it out using air chisels.

Port bow

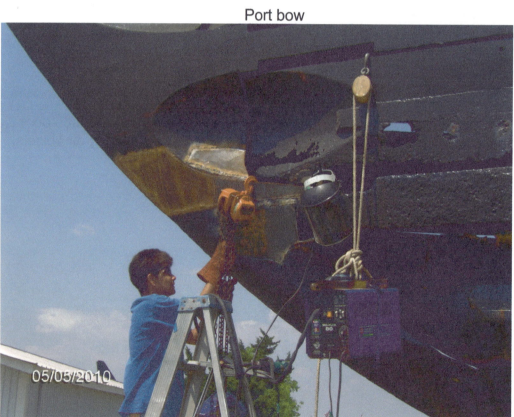

Lesley getting ready to bend metal

Almost done, note new numbers

Port bow done

June
Started rebuilding stern. Cut out rusted hull and sand blasted and painted inside. Welded new piece on upper hull, started on top door. Cleaned up boat for crew reunion, Joe and Eileen

Leffrado polished everything inside for the reunion. The reunion was again a special time, 7 crew made it this year and many of the families, the reunions are getting harder each year knowing the crew won't be around much longer. The boat seems to know they are coming back, it feels different inside.

Phillip Williamson (Willie) 3-13, David Schmidt 12,13, Bill Lister 9-13, Gainey Maxwell 14, Bob White 2-12, Donald Kronholm (Swede) 8-12

Crew reunion 2010

For the reunion we pushed one of MK 27 torpedoes out tube #7 and told the crew we didn't have enough air pressure to clear the tube.

Stanley Tools donated tools and supplies to us from a tour I gave to Paul Zarlengo, including grinders and wheels, welding gloves and a 120v welder, air drills and drill bits, screw drivers, socket set and pry bars. Tools were from Dewalt, Mac and Proto, all a huge help.

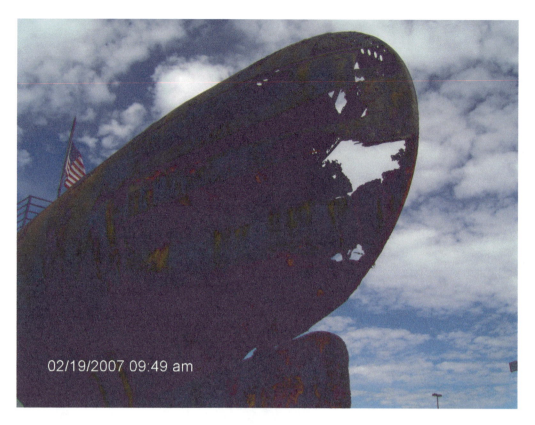

Starting port stern

Working shutter doors in place

Sand blasted inside stern while open. We called the platform our dance floor.

Almost done, the chain fall was used to haul welders to platform

Primed, trying to duplicate the pink submarine

Lesley putting finishing touches on port stern

Port stern done

August thru November
Sand blasted and painted the port side. We had not done the port super structure so it took longer than the starboard side. NES Rental let us have a man lift at reduced cost which was a big help and when we went to turn it in we found out the park had picked up the rental without telling us. We used 57 tons of sand this year.

Sand blasting the port side

The forward end is slow going due to the height of the super structure

We blast and prime as much as we can in the morning each day, starting at 0530. On Friday we top coat what we primed for the week.

We can finally see the stern. We had to make a gate in the fence to get access to the back with the equipment.

Finished

When we went into the field to look and take this photo, we could not believe we had repaired, blasted and painted the port side in one summer.

The small details

December
We cleaned the inside of the boat and recovered from the summer's work.

January 2011
Scrapped and painted the crew's washroom and head in preparation for bringing the washing machine on board that we got from the USS Pampanito. The serial numbers are very close to the one the Drum had in 1945, wonder where it went.

Crew's Head

Crew's Head

February
We moved the washing machine in by taking it all apart and then putting it back together inside the washroom, lots of fun and a lot of time standing on our heads. Than we re-installed the sink in the CPO quarters that had been removed in 1964. A guy found it in his garage, contacted us and sent it back.

Putting the washing machine back together

The washing machine finished, wish we could use it

Chief Petty Officers sink, back home

March
Cleaned boat for Navy inspection. Than did our normal deck repairs and fixed the engine room hatch. Lesley chipped and painted it and the hatch trunk and I replaced the wood in the after gun mount.

Aft engine room hatch

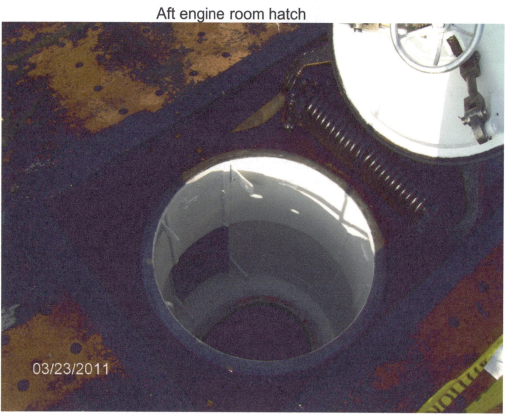

Engine room hatch and trunk painted

Engine room hatch

Aft gun mount with old wood

Aft gun mount with new wood and painted

April
We cleaned all the sand out of the water ways on the tank tops. We cut a big hole in the dent in tank 7B and went inside and knocked rust off. We found the bottoms of the I beams be gone from rust. I than cut holes in several other tanks and pumped the water out to check the beams in them. They appear to be in better shape, Went to O'Neal Steel and they donated 18 11' pieces of I beam.

I beams in the bottom of #7 fuel tank, port side, we were told we didn't need to worry about the tanks

May

We painted the deck with the help of two volunteers that served on the USS Corporal.

Starboard side primed

The volunteers painting, being filmed by the newspaper videographer

June
We got ready for the crew reunion. Again we only had five crew that could make it but it was great and our curator got great video interviews with them. After the reunion I went to Charleston, SC for a James Madison reunion, also great.

Bill Lister 9-13, Gerard DeRosa (Skinney Ghinney) 6-10, Phillip Williamson (Willie) 3-13, Bob White 2-12, David Schmidt 12,13

Crew reunion 2011 with the crewmates

July-
Started working inside tank #7, port side first, replaced the 10 bottom I beams, then moved to the starboard side because we were getting flooded from heavy afternoon rains.

This is the inside of #7b, the port side, after we first opened it. And before we sand blasted.

Inside #7 normal fuel tank

After sand blasting we could see just how bad it was. O'Neal steel had already donated the new I beams, we wanted to have them on hand first so we could get some support in as soon as possible.

Here we have started replacing the beams. There is about 30" of space between the pressure hull and the fuel tank skin.

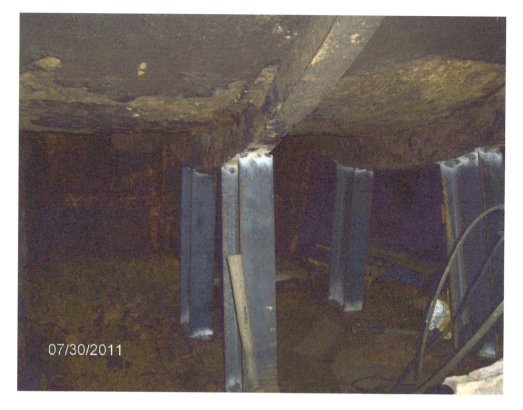

This is the starboard side of the tank looking aft. We didn't sand blast it but air chiseled of the rust where we were going to cut, mainly to save sand.

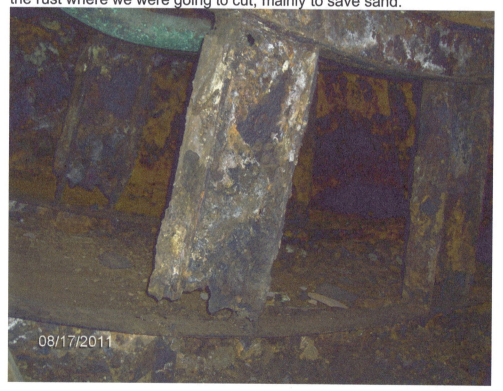

After we have replaced some of the I beams.

We discovered that the longitudinal frames and the ring frames on the tank skin were gone also in the bottom 6' of the tank.

One new longitudinal frame.

This is how we made the ring frames. I used an old work mate bench to bend the flange to the web.

New ring frames in place and the skin removed that was full of holes.

New skin in place, starting to look a lot better.

Inside looking at the new frames and skin.

We moved back to the port side to start removing the dented area.

An inside look at the dent.

The dent from the inside

The first piece of new skin. We had to work in sections to try to preserve as much strength as possible. We would not cut out any frames until Monday mornings to be sure we could get support in in the same week.

The lower portion of the ring frames

The longitudinal frames are gone too.

Another big piece of the dent removed along with the ring frames.

New 8' section of ring frame, this was a challenge to make and get lined up with the good part of the skin. Note the string.

A new piece of skin. This was the largest single piece we have put on the boat and presented new challenges.

I am cutting out another frame

Lesley is welding in the new frame.

Another piece of the puzzle.

The port side dent repairs when we stopped for the winter.

We moved inside for the winter and discussed which compartment we would repaint. Lesley said the aft bulkhead in the forward torpedo room was really bothering her, so with that comment it was decided. Lesley started with the overhead and hull and I tackled the bulkhead because I could fit in the pit under the step going into forward battery.
The main goal was to scrape the loose paint and get rid of the red and yellow which were not the original colors and to paint the hull and bulkheads white instead of the cold water pea green. During WWII most of the piping wasn't painted, it is copper, but we just didn't have the time to scrape and clean all the pipes so we decided to scrape the loose paint and paint them light grey. The wiring also wasn't painted but there just wasn't any way to chip the paint of and clean them up so we painted the wiring white.

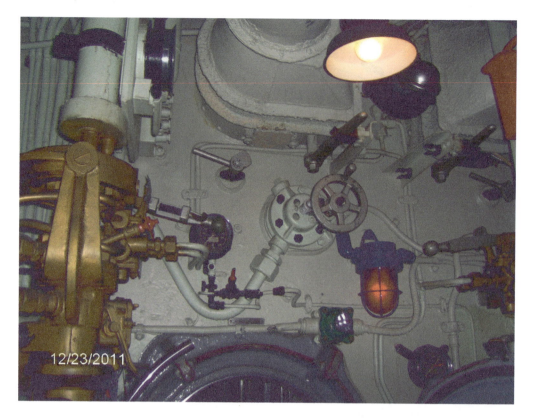

The aft bulkhead above the watertight door going into forward battery.

The step going into forward battery and the pit underneath between the sonar heads. I spent three weeks in there, a two foot deep space.

A before photo of the aft bulkhead

The aft pit.

The aft bulkhead below deck level.

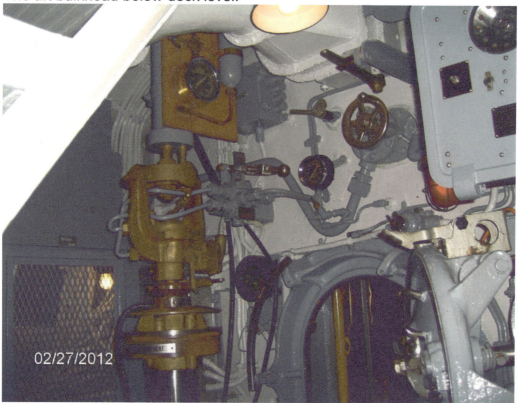

The after photo

After photo of the pit

Lesley spent over a week in the officer's head

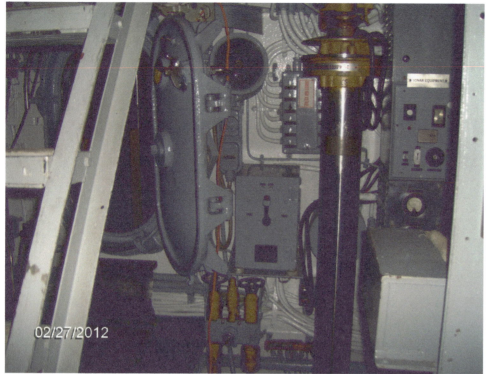
Aft bulkhead

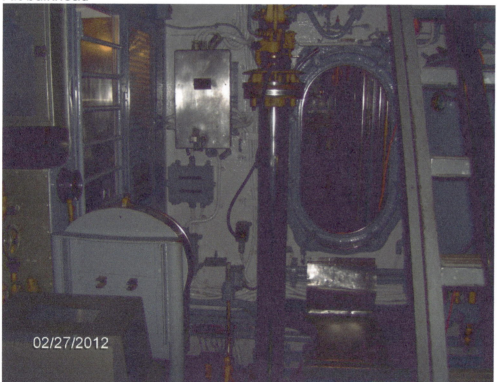
Looking aft in the forward torpedo room

The lower level in the forward room (also called the pit)

The port side of the pit

Forward torpedo tubes

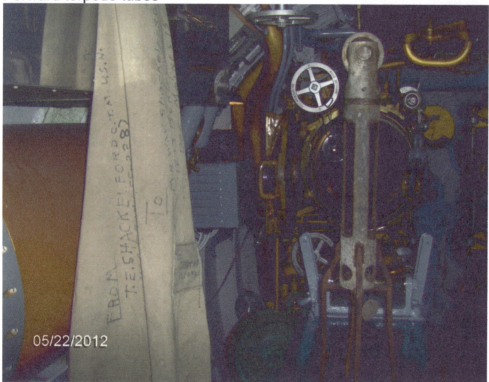
A sea bag donated by a crewman's family
When the weather warmed up in the spring we moved back outside and did some more repair work on the port side dent, started on the fuel compensating tank and our USS Corporal shipmates returned for four days and we had them sand and prime the props, than Lesley and I painted them bronze.

Corporal crew

Dent repair

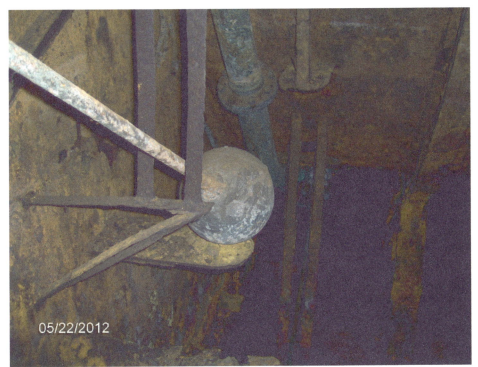
Fuel compensating tank. These are ball floats to give level, there are six in this tank and the fuel expansion tank on the port side.

The two I beams in the center need to be replaced

New I beams, we also replaced one horizontal beam

Putting new skin on the fuel compensating tank.

New skin in place

It is time for this year's reunion, the 41st, so we cleaned ourselves up and the boat.

Drum crew l-r Gerard DeRosa patrols 6-10 (aka Skinney Ghinny), Gainey Maxwell patrol 14, Phillip Williamson patrols 3-13 (aka Willie), David Schmidt patrols 12-14, Donald Kronholm patrols 8-12 (aka Swede)

The crew and family members. As always the reunion was great, lots of sea stories, some new ones even and a good time, but it is really sad when it is over.

After the reunion I emailed the Director of the museum boat program for the Navy and told him we were getting ready to sand blast and paint in the tanks and that we needed to move the lead ballast. I asked if we had to put it back. I received the reply stating no go ahead and sell it and use the money for the restoration. This is the answer I was hoping for. I contacted scrap dealers and found one that gave the best price and two people to help get it out. I then went to the park commissioners and they agreed to all the money going to the Drum restoration. The lead is in 50 and 100 pound bricks and in six tanks.

We started pumping water out of the tanks, cutting holes in the bottom to be able to clean out the mud and figuring out how to move the lead. We hung one of our electric hoists in the tank from chains and experimented. I made tongs, like an ice tong and these worked really good. In July we started pulling lead and in seven days removed forty six tons from tanks 4 & 5 and stopped to get tanks 6 cleaned out, they still had a lot of mud and oil. We also had the area under three tanks dug out so we could sand blast the bottom of the hull and cut bigger holes to drop the lead out the bottom of tanks 6. Tanks 6 have the air bottles in them and were coated with cold plastic which had melted and run down covering the bottom layer of lead. We had to chisel off the plastic with an air chisel to cut the straps holding the lead and to be able to pry the lead loose. Almost every brick had to be pried loose with a hammer and thin pry bar because they were fused to each other and the hull and stuck with mud, oil and plastic.

The scrap people came back in August and we got the lead out of tanks 6a and 6c, (starboard side), another 20 tons. We had to cancel the port side due to hurricane Isaac approach. Following are photos of the inside of the tanks with the lead.

4a

4a

5a

5a

5b

MBT 4b

MBT5a

5b

5b

5b

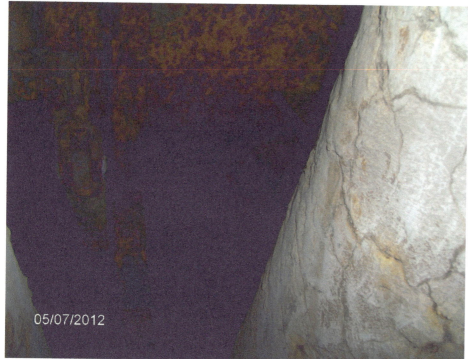
MBT6a

MBT6b

6b

MBT6c

6c

MBT6d

6d

The scrap people came back in September and we finished removing the lead from the port side tanks. We took out 37.2 tons for a total of 83.5 tons and were paid a total of $100,288. We are now figuring out how to clean out the cold plastic coating in the ballast tanks so we can have them sand blasted. We are thinking of trying a steam cleaner.

We tried a hot water pressure washer which worked fairly well but made a bigger mess so it is back to air chisel and putting it in plastic garbage bags and carrying it out, not fun.

We cut holes in the rest of the tanks we haven't opened so the sand blasters could get in and we could get the sand out. In MBT 2A, B, C, and D we found more lead, initial guess another 20 tons. So it was back to air chiseling plastic and cutting straps. We spent all summer, June thru November cleaning out the tanks, removing lead, cleaning more tanks and in December started pulling lead from MBT 2B and D and were delayed a couple of times due to weather. We got all of 2D and almost all of 2B and had almost 18 tons. We took off over the Christmas/New Year week and went back to it in January, I had really hoped to be done with the lead last year.

Chiseling out plastic getting ready to cut straps

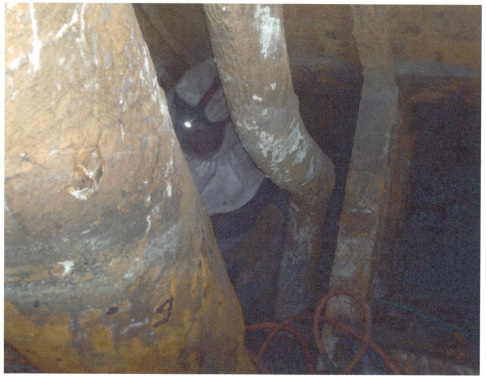

Lots of room in this one

Cutting straps

Nice and clean also

This worried Lesley a little but I was just trying to get warm

Getting in and out of the tanks is lots of fun also

The second week of January 2013 we got the scrap people to come back and we removed the lead from the starboard side of #2 MBT's, it came to 16 tons for a total of 116 tons. These tanks were unusually hard to remove the lead because the ship yard had put in multiple layers of strapping and plates to hold the lead in place, and packed it in tighter.

January and February 2013

After we finished removing the lead we went in the tanks and started cutting out the rest of the straps and supports and bulkheads that held the lead. I would then go in and scoop the sand, mud and rust up, put in a 2 ½ gal bucket, drag it up to the hole in the hull and dump it, then when it was cleaned out, cut a hole in the bottom and wash out the tank. The last two weeks of February I rented a mini-backhoe and we dug out from under the tanks where the space had filled in and put up steel bulkheads to keep it from filling in again. We had to use a 12' piece of I beam to shove into the mud, pull it out, shovel the mud off and repeat. We dug out the rudder and put a drain line and lined it all with rock.

Lesley running the front end loader digging out the mud

March 2013
The weather turned to winter off and on so we would work in the tanks when it was warm enough and go inside when it turned cold, windy and rainy.

April 2013
The first week I came down with a bad cold which turned into bronchitis so I stayed home and worked on this book. We finally got word that the dvds for the movie USS Seaviper are done so we should have them next week.

May 2013
We continued to clean out tanks and started making new frames to replace the bad ones.

June 2013
We painted the deck inside the boat, staying late one night and replaced broken tiles, Cleaned and polished to get ready for the crew reunion. The reunion was great as usual with the same five that was here last year. Gainey Maxwell had trouble with his camper but we were able to get him fixed up at East Bay Automotive who would not charge him for the work they did, great people. The crew presented the Holland Club certificates to three of Mobile Bay Base members.
At the banquet on Friday night at the Oyster House, we had almost the entire crew from the Park's gift shop and it was a great time. Ralph, Rob and Lynanne from Mighty Moments, the people who filmed USS Seaviper arrived on Saturday night to film for two days on the Drum for the documentary they are making.

Donald Kronholm Patrols 8-12, Gainey Maxwell Patrol 14, Gerard DeRosa Patrols 6-10, David Schmidt Patrols 12-14, Phillip Williamson Patrols 3-13

We will continue to clean out the tanks getting them ready to sand blast and start doing the repair work of the interior framing and replacing the skin of the tanks.

To follow our progress go to www.drum228.org and the restoration page where the story will continue.

Made in the USA
Columbia, SC
11 July 2024

38363430R00137